30-SECOND
ANCIENT ROME

30-SECOND
ANCIENT ROME

The 50 most important
achievements of a timeless
civilization, each explained in
half a minute

Editor
Matthew Nicholls

Contributors
Luke Houghton
Ailsa Hunt
Peter Kruschwitz
Dunstan Lowe
Annalisa Marzano
Matthew Nicholls
Susanne Turner

METRO BOOKS
NEW YORK

METRO BOOKS
New York

An Imprint of Sterling Publishing
387 Park Avenue South
New York, NY 10016

© 2014 by Ivy Press Limited

This book was conceived,
designed, and produced by
Ivy Press
210 High Street, Lewes,
East Sussex BN7 2NS, U.K.
www.ivypress.co.uk

Creative Director **Peter Bridgewater**
Publisher **Susan Kelly**
Editorial Director **Caroline Earle**
Art Director **Michael Whitehead**
Project Editor **Jamie Pumfrey**
Designer **Ginny Zeal**
Illustrator **Ivan Hissey**
Glossaries Text **Matthew Nicholls**

ISBN-13: 978-1-4351-5179-6

For information about custom editions,
special sales, and premium and corporate
purchases, please contact Sterling Special
Sales at 800-805-5489 or specialsales@
sterlingpublishing.com.

Manufactured in China
Color origination by Ivy Press Reprographics

2 4 6 8 10 9 7 5 3 1

www.sterlingpublishing.com

CONTENTS

INTRODUCTION
Matthew Nicholls

Marcus Tullius Cicero, Roman statesman, philosopher, lawyer, and scholar. Remembered as one of the greatest orators and his writings are the epitome of Roman Prose.

Traces of the huge Roman empire remain all over Europe, from northern Britain to Syria and the coast of north Africa. Anyone who walks the length of Hadrian's Wall, for example, following it for the 80 miles (130 km) or so from coast to coast through the windswept countryside of northern England, is traveling through what was once a far-flung Roman frontier. Yet even here, hundreds of miles north of Rome's Mediterranean heartland, there is much of Rome in evidence. The Wall itself, and its string of neat, symmetrical forts, with characteristic bathhouses and headquarters buildings, speak of the power and organization of the Roman army, and its formidable architectural and technological capacity—and also of Rome's desire to impose itself on new territory, by force if necessary. In and around these outposts, finds of pottery, coins, clothing, altars, and even private letters show how the soldiers and settlers brought with them ways of living, eating, trading, worshipping, thinking, and writing that began to transform Britain—along with many other parts of Europe, north Africa and the Middle East—into a Roman province, leaving a lasting legacy. Such small finds from this great military monument also remind us that historical events are made up from thousands of smaller, private, stories.

This picture is repeated at hundreds of sites, military and civilian, public and private, all over the empire. We also have a rich body of surviving literature from Roman times, transmitted over the centuries in copies of copies—so we can set Hadrian's Wall in its context by reading what ancient historical writers and poets said about Rome's conquest of Britain. From epic poetry to history, from speeches to medical treatises to recipes, this rich body of literature allows scholars to explore very different aspects of Rome's long and colorful history—and newly discovered texts are still turning up, in the dry sands of Egypt, in carbonized books from Herculaneum, and in old libraries.

This study reveals a fascinating people. At times the Romans can seem similar to us, with their concern for home comforts—central

The Roman empire still imposes on to the modern world with Hadrian's wall, the defensive fortification in northern England, cutting its way across the landscape nearly 2000 years since its creation.

heating, proper water supplies, and drains—and their passion for urban life, for good communications, for fine food and wine, for literature, entertainment, and status. But they were also very different. Think of slavery and gladiatorial combat, their world of gods and sacrifices and worship of the living emperor. The grand statues and monuments that filled their public spaces set the mold for many modern cities, but speak of a triumphalism that has now fallen from fashion. In truth, the Romans were both familiar and foreign, which makes the study of their lives and times endlessly fascinating. The contributors to this book ably and enthusiastically take on the challenge of bringing to vivid life the very best and the worst of this ambitious, inventive, cultured, and at times brutal and licentious episode in western history.

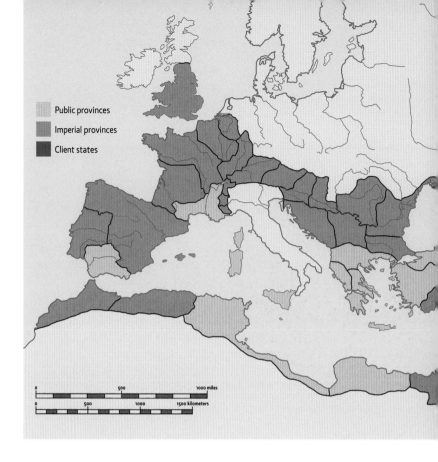

Public provinces
Imperial provinces
Client states

| 0 | 500 | 1000 miles |
| 0 | 500 | 1000 | 1500 kilometers |

753 BCE Foundation of Rome
Legendary foundation date—but, according to some modern archaeology, not far off the mark.

509 BCE Formation of Roman republic
Expulsion of the last of Rome's kings: a new republican constitution delivered safeguards against excessive individual power.

fifth–third C BCE Growth of Roman power
Roman power spread across Italy through warfare and treaties.

264–146 BCE Punic Wars
A series of three draining wars against Carthage, Rome's greatest rival; final victory allowed Rome's Mediterranean empire to expand.

ca.133–44 BCE Crisis of the republic
A period of unrest and repeated civil war, as Rome's republican constitution struggled to contain imperial expansion, individual political ambition, and inequality.

60–53 BCE "First triumvirate"
Political alliance of three of Rome's greatest figures: Caesar, Pompey, and Crassus.

March 15th, 44 BCE Death of Julius Caesar
Rome's dictator felled by senators resentful of his dominance, triggering further civil war.

31 BCE–14 CE Reign of Augustus
Rome's first emperor. Expansion and consolidation of empire; foundation of a long-lived system of one-man rule.

An overview of Roman history

The history of ancient Rome lasted well over a thousand years, from its legendary foundation on April 21st 753 BCE through to the fall of the (western) Roman empire on September 4th 476 CE. Its empire covered much of Europe and parts of north Africa and the Middle East. Its legacy in almost every area of human activity remains to the present day.

This huge span of geography and history can be hard to navigate, but the timeline here shows some major landmarks in Roman history and provides a framework of reference for the rest of the book. Likewise the map, which shows the empire at its greatest extent in the early second century CE, locates Rome itself and charts the Mediterranean world in which its influence eventually spread from the draughty outpost marked by Hadrian's Wall to the borders of modern Iraq.

31 BCE–68 CE Julio-Claudian dynasty of emperors
Augustus, Tiberius, Caligula, Claudius, and Nero.

68–97 CE Flavian dynasty
Vespasian, Titus, and Domitian.

98–117 CE Reign of Trajan
Rome's "best emperor;" under his rule, the empire reached its fullest geographical extent.

96–192 CE Adoptive/Antonine emperors
Nerva, Trajan, Hadrian, Antoninus Pius, Marcus Aurelius, Lucius Verus, and Commodus were emperor by adoption, rather than the transmission of power from father to a son: a largely stable, prosperous period.

193–235 CE Severan Dynasty
A dynasty of African emperors who came to power after a period of civil war.

235–284 CE Third-century crisis
Short-lived emperors, inflation, plague, invasion, discord, and rebellion.

293–313 CE Tetrarchy
Diocletian's new system of rule by four emperors, which helped to put an end to crisis.

306–337 CE Rule of Constantine
Rome's first Christian emperor; founded Constantinople (Byzantium) as an eastern capital.

476 CE End of western Roman empire
Waves of invaders brought the western empire to its knees but the eastern empire of Byzantium survived until 1453.

How this book works

In university departments across the world, specialist classicists and ancient historians cover very diverse aspects of Rome's life and legacy, studying language and literature, history, art and architecture, and archaeology. The seven chapters of this book aim, very broadly, to explore these key areas.

Compressing this richness into just 50, single-page, topics was difficult, but my hope is that readers will find here both the familiar— legions, gladiators, aqueducts, emperors—as well as new concepts, such as rhetoric, divination, and the way Romans treated people in death as well as in life, suggesting something of the fascinating wealth of material that the archaeological and written records provide.

Each entry is, like Caesar's Gaul, divided into three parts. The main 30-second history sets out the topic at hand. In a single sentence, the 3-second summary offers a quick synopsis, while a separate panel, the 3-minute excavation, provides a further aspect or something to ponder on. You can dip in and out of the chapters or read them through; each one is prefaced by a glossary to help with unfamiliar terminology and concepts. There are also profiles, one per chapter, of key individuals who, in their time, proved highly influential on society at large, beginning with Caesar himself.

The first chapter, **Land & State**, opens with the legendary foundation of Rome, and charts its political development from kingdom to republic to empire; it ends with a look at the famous legions that powered Rome's rise from city-state to global capital. **People & Society** explores aspects of the way Roman society operated, from the status and interrelation of citizens and slaves, men and women, to the framework of law and governance that bound the empire together. **Roman Life** considers some of the ways in which these people lived and worked; the fabric of the ordinary and economic life is increasingly as much of interest to ancient historians as the emperors and elite. The succeeding chapters, **Language & Literature** and **Thought & Belief**, show us how Roman society spoke,

Augustus, the founder of the Roman empire and its first emperor. Best known for the huge expansion that enlarged the empire, but was successful in reforming taxes, developing road networks and rebuilding much of the city of Rome.

thought, and wrote about itself. The final chapters, **Architecture, Monuments & Art** and **Buildings & Technology** reveal the practical side of Roman achievement, its temples, circuses, mosaics, bathhouses, and roads whose monumental remains—like Hadrian's Wall—cannot fail to captivate and impress the traveler. All roads led to Rome, and we hope that this book will also take you there, by a variety of different routes.

LAND & STATE

LAND & STATE
GLOSSARY

Aeneid An epic poem in 12 books composed by Rome's greatest poet, Virgil, with the backing of Augustus. An instant classic, it tells of the wanderings of Aeneas, a Trojan prince who flees the ruins of Troy to travel to Italy and found the Roman people.

army terms The Roman army's composition and strength varied over time, but during much of the Roman empire it fielded a total of about 30 legions. Each legion consisted of heavy infantry legionary soldiers and non-citizen auxiliary troops who were levied from one of Rome's allies and could use a variety of weapons and tactics. There would also be a wing of mounted cavalry troops. Each legion contained a small cadre of senior officers and a number of tactical subdivisions: ten cohorts (except the double-strength first cohort) containing six centuries of 80 men each, commanded by centurions. At the lowest level of command legionaries were organized into eight-man tent parties each called a *contubernium*, commanded by a *decanus*. The whole system helped to foster comradeship and a sense of unit and legion loyalty.

auctoritas Unofficial power based on personality and ability to compel respect, rather than an official title or office. An important basis of the first emperor Augustus's long reign.

cavalry *See* **army terms**

cohort, century *See* **army terms**

consul The top magistrate of the Roman republic; each year two were elected, to keep each other in check.

Dacia An eastern Roman province in what is now Romania, finally conquered by Trajan. An important source of metal ore.

Gaul An area of Roman imperial rule covering present-day France, western Switzerland, northern Italy, Belgium, Luxembourg, and western Germany. Its conquest was completed by Julius Caesar in the 50s BCE. The region was divided into several Roman provinces and remained within the empire until its dissolution centuries later.

gladius Double-edged, pointed sword carried by legionaries; replaced in the later empire by the longer *spatha*.

Iberia The peninsula containing modern Spain and Portugal was conquered by Rome during the Punic Wars and divided into the various provinces of Roman Hispania from 197 BCE.

imperator A title spontaneously bestowed by victorious Roman troops on their commanding general; eventually became part of the titulature of the Roman emperors. It also refers to the *imperium* or formal power possessed by a Roman magistrate.

Latium The region of central Italy where Rome was founded; home of the Latins.

legionary *See* **army terms**

Republic Work of fourth-century BCE Greek philosophy by Plato, which discusses the idea of justice and different forms of government. Includes the idea of an ideal state governed by philosopher-kings.

pilum (pl. pila) Iron-tipped wooden javelin; each Roman legionary carried two *pila* to hurl at the enemy in battle.

plebeian order, plebs The non-patrician citizenry of Rome. Initially excluded from power, they won equality and political representation by 287 BCE through the "conflict of the orders," a two-century long struggle in which they threatened to leave Rome altogether if their demands were not met.

Punic Wars A series of three bitter wars between Rome and Carthage (a powerful rival state on the coast of North Africa), fought in the third to second centuries BCE, culminating with the fall and sack of Carthage in 146 BCE.

princeps A Latin word that translates roughly as "first citizen." A word to refer to the emporer.

principate Name for the system of one-man rule established by Augustus, Rome's first emperor or *princeps*.

Saeptimontium A religious festival involving Rome's "seven" (*septem*) or possibly "fortified" (*saepti*) hills (*montes*)—although the selection of hills does not include the seven usually thought of as the most important.

Rubicon River A small river in northeast Italy. Famous only for being the first-century BCE boundary of Italy: Julius Caesar committed an act of civil war when he crossed the river with his army.

scutum A legionary's shield. Typically a curved rectangle with a central boss and carrying handles.

FOUNDATION

the 30-second history

Romulus and Remus were the twin sons of the war-god Mars and a mortal princess. Condemned (like the young Moses) by a jealous male relative to abandonment by the river, the babies were saved by miraculous interventions, suckled by a wolf, and rescued by a kindly shepherd and his wife. Grown to adulthood, they discovered their ancestry and chose to found a new city. In a quarrel over its proper site, Romulus killed Remus and named his city after himself, founding a dynasty of kings that lasted until their overthrow inaugurated the Republic. Many elements of this unsettling story pointed forward to aspects of Roman history and identity—military toughness (sons of Mars, nourished by a wolf) but also a capacity for civil war and violence (the brothers' quarrel). Archaeology tells its own story. The site of Rome seems to have been inhabited at the dawn of the Iron Age, around the tenth to ninth centuries BCE, a period in which Rome was a meeting place between growing powerblocks in Etrutria, Latium, and Samnium. Evidence of ninth-century BCE settlement on the Palatine Hill resonates with the traditional belief that Romulus founded the city here in 753 BCE.

3-SECOND SURVEY
Rome's legendary foundation story is a myth, but one firmly embedded in Roman identity that appears to echo aspects of historical truth supported by the archaeological record.

3-MINUTE EXCAVATION
Romans told various versions of this story. One traced Romulus's ancestry back farther to Aeneas, a Trojan prince fleeing the sack of Troy, who eventually reached the future site of Rome after toiling round the Mediterranean: this was the subject of Virgil's epic poem, the *Aeneid*. Roman historical imagination was happy to accommodate these myths alongside the earliest strands of Rome's recorded history, identifying sacred places in the city where they were thought to have occurred.

RELATED HISTORIES
See also
SITE OF ROME
page 18

REPUBLICAN GOVERNMENT
page 20

VIRGIL
page 84

3-SECOND BIOGRAPHIES
AENEAS
Son of the Trojan lord Anchises and the goddess Aphrodite. A bit part in Homer's *Iliad*, he is center stage in the Roman epic the *Aeneid*, where he travels to Italy to found the Roman race

FAUSTULUS
Shepherd who, with his wife Acca Larentia, found and raised the abandoned twins

RHEA SILVIA
Daughter of King Numitor of Alba Longa, an ancient city near Rome, and mother of Romulus and Remus

30-SECOND TEXT
Matthew Nicholls

The truth of Rome's legends may not bear scrutiny, but the city takes its name from its most famous son.

SITE OF ROME

the 30-second history

Rome is, famously, a city of seven hills but which seven is open to interpretation; there are actually well over a dozen. What is clear is that Rome owes much of its character and fortune to its location. Important land routes converge here and travelers between Etruria, Latium, and Campania could cross the river Tiber at Tiber Island. The river is also navigable down to the sea 18 miles (30 km) away at Ostia, making the site a crucial interchange for trade across and beyond Italy. The city's hills—spurs whose sides have been cut away by tributary streams flowing to the river—offered security, fresh air in summer, and building rock (a rather crumbly brown tufa); they became the nucleus of early separate village communities. The intervening valley land provided meeting and trading places which, when drained and paved, turned into Rome's forum spaces. After Rome's hilltop villages had joined together into a single city, the individual hills retained characters and traditions of their own. The Capitoline, Rome's religious stronghold, housed the great Temple of the "Capitoline Triad"; the Palatine remained a site for aristocratic villas, while the Aventine for a long time was associated with the plebeian order.

RELATED HISTORIES
See also
FOUNDATION
page 16

TRADE & INDUSTRY
page 58

THE FORUM
page 122

AQUEDUCTS & SEWERS
page 150

3-SECOND SURVEY
The hills and valleys of Rome, located at a crucial transport crossroads, acquired legendary and historical associations and shaped the city's destiny.

3-MINUTE EXCAVATION
A Roman city religious festival called the "saeptimontium" may be an early reference to the seven hills (*montes*) of Rome—but eight "hills" participated in it, not including the Capitoline, Aventine, Quirinal, or Viminal, four of the city's biggest. The seven-headed beast of the Book of Revelation may be another reference to the seven-hilled city; and many cities around the world, from Durham and Torquay in England to Constantinople, Moscow, Seattle, Kampala, and Thiruvananthapuram in India have all claimed to share this characteristic geography.

3-SECOND BIOGRAPHY
TARQUINIUS PRISCUS
579 BCE
Fifth of Rome's legendary kings, credited with overseeing the draining of the marshy forum area with Rome's Great Sewer, the Cloaca Maxima

30-SECOND TEXT
Matthew Nicholls

Sited near the mouth of the Tiber, Rome was ideally placed for trade with its Mediterranean neighbors and—by virtue of its many hills—easily defended.

REPUBLICAN GOVERNMENT

the 30-second history

In the beginning Rome was ruled by kings. By the sixth century BCE the city's aristocracy was tiring of its Etruscan monarchs, who had developed a reputation for authoritarian arrogance. In 509 BCE an uprising against Tarquinius Superbus replaced the monarchy with a republican government, which developed into a complicated republican constitution. For commentators like Polybius this was an interesting and powerful fusion of different types of government: at the top was a pair of king-like chief magistrates—consuls—but their powers were tempered by having to share office and by holding it only for a year. There was also an oligarchic senate, comprised of men from Rome's leading families, and some democratizing elements including elections to magistracies and citizen assemblies with legislative and warmaking powers. This constitution functioned for nearly five centuries, accommodating dissent such as the threatened secession of Rome's plebeians, winning major wars, and presiding over a huge expansion of Roman territorial power. Eventually it grew unstable: enriched and emboldened by the booty of conquest, successful politician-generals sought more power than Rome had been prepared to give to any one man, and popular unrest was rife. Enter Julius Caesar.

3-SECOND SURVEY
Rome's republican constitution allowed it to grow to superpower status, but faltered and failed under pressure in the first century BCE.

3-MINUTE EXCAVATION
Rome's republican government survived as long as it did by combining respect for precedent and the law with a flexible response to new problems. As city and empire grew, new magistracies were created to deal with the administration. When Rome conquered provinces, ex-magistrates went to govern them. When the lower orders threatened revolt, they were granted special magistrates (tribunes) to represent their interests. And in times of crisis a dictator could be appointed for a limited period.

RELATED HISTORY
See also
IMPERIAL GOVERNMENT
page 24

3-SECOND BIOGRAPHIES
TARQUINIUS SUPERBUS
ca. 535–495 BCE
Legendary seventh and final king of Rome, whose overthrow resulted in the establishment of the republic

LUCRETIA
ca. 510 BCE
Roman matron whose rape by Sextus, son of Tarquinius Superbus, outraged Rome and led to the overthrow of the monarchy

POLYBIUS
ca. 200–118 BCE
A Greek taken to Rome as an honored captive, where he wrote a history of the rise of the Roman state

30-SECOND TEXT
Matthew Nicholls

Growing political instability in the republic set the stage for Julius Caesar to usher in a new era.

100 BCE
Born into aristocratic Roman family, the Iulii

70s–60s BCE
Climbs up the political ranks, aided by lavish games funded by borrowing (to be repaid by the plunder of conquest)

62 BCE
Praetor in Rome and then governor in Spain—wins a military triumph but forfeits it to stand for election to consul, the highest-ranking magistrate

59 BCE
Elected Consul. Rules in alliance with Crassus and Pompey as "First Triumvirate"

58–51 BCE
Conquest of Gaul; Caesar seeks to return to Rome on his own terms

49 BCE
Crosses Rubicon river, an act of defiance leading to civil war

48 BCE
Defeats Pompey (now an enemy) and chases him to Egypt, where Pompey is killed. Begins alliance with Cleopatra

46 BCE
Caesar, now unchallenged, is loaded with honors in Rome, suggesting lasting autocracy

March 15th, 44 BCE
Frustrated conspirators stab Caesar to death at a senate meeting

JULIUS CAESAR

Julius Caesar is one of the most famous names in history. The title "Caesar" was held by centuries of Roman emperors after him, and became synonymous with autocratic power worldwide—the Russian "Tsar" and the German "Kaiser" both derive from his name.

Caesar's personal charm, brilliance, and shrewd self-presentation won him wide popular appeal, challenging the boundaries of the old republican constitution whose overlapping and annually renewed magistracies were designed to keep individuals from attaining too much power.

In his youth Caesar weathered stormy times, including foreign military campaigns, a civil war between his patron Marius and the dictator Sulla, and being kidnapped by pirates (whom he later pursued and crucified). Military success in Spain and clever politicking at home brought him to the top magistracy, the consulship, in 59 BCE; with his colleagues Pompey and Crassus he pursued a populist brand of politics, which threatened elements of Rome's senatorial aristocracy.

His conquest of Gaul during the 50s BCE allowed him to seek more personal power than the republican state was prepared to give him: ordered to lay down his arms, Caesar refused and in 49 BCE moved his army— by this time permanently loyal to him as commander— across the Rubicon river, thereby breaking an ancient prohibition on bringing troops into Italy: an act that initiated civil war.

Caesar emerged as victor after various adventures, including his dalliance with Cleopatra in Egypt, and was made "dictator in perpetuity," pursuing a varied program of political reform.

Caesar's divisive rule ended with his assassination by a group of senators on the Ides of March 44 BCE. Following a further civil war, his legacy was secured by the triumph of his great-nephew and heir Augustus, founder of a long line of emperors.

The largely positive way in which later generations viewed Caesar was partly due to the influence of his written works. A writer and orator of brilliance, Caesar left accounts of his campaigns in Gaul, and of the subsequent civil war, which were intended to influence contemporary opinion and, in all likelihood, the judgment of posterity. His account of the *Gallic Wars* is a favorite of classics students today for its clear and lucid Latin and exciting subject matter.

Matthew Nicholls

IMPERIAL GOVERNMENT

the 30-second history

Out of the wreckage of the Roman republic Julius Caesar, and then Augustus, crafted a new system of rule by a single autocratic figure whom we call the "emperor." However, there was not (at least at first) any real constitutional position or single title of "emperor." Augustus actually ruled through an accumulation of traditional republican offices and powers under the pretence of having restored the old state rather than supplanted it—and his successors followed suit. In reality it was Augustus's own personal *auctoritas* and his defeat of all rivals that allowed him to rule practically unchallenged and pass on his power to a line of successors claiming descent from him. By the time this Julio-Claudian dynasty died out with Nero, the imperial system was too embedded to be removed, and carried on through successive dynasties—Flavians, Antonines, Severans—until the overthrow of the last child-emperor, Romulus Augustulus, in 476 CE. Along the way there were various interruptions, from assassinations, usurpations, and civil wars to Diocletian's attempt to divide the empire into eastern and western halves, each ruled by a pair of senior and junior emperors (the tetrarchy), but no credible alternative to the rule of emperors ever emerged.

3-SECOND SURVEY
Rule by a single emperor placed unprecedented and enormous power, for good or ill, in the hands of a single individual.

3-MINUTE EXCAVATION
Mindful of Rome's ancient fear of monarchy, Augustus assembled a series of offices, powers, and honors left over from the republican constitution —consul, chief priest, imperator, and a complex magisterial privilege called "tribunician power." This ad hoc arrangement was handed to emperor after emperor, but the ambiguity of autocratic rule through republican powers left room for challenge—the role of emperor could be passed to a blood relative or adoptive heir, but also could be challenged, usurped, or divided.

RELATED HISTORY
See also
REPUBLICAN GOVERNMENT
page 20

3-SECOND BIOGRAPHIES
CALIGULA
12–41 CE
Emperor (37–41 CE) epitomized how the system could pass enormous power into unsuitable hands

TRAJAN
53–117 CE
Emperor (98–117 CE), military leader, fair-minded politician, prolific builder: hailed as the "best emperor."

ELAGABALUS
203–222 CE
Spectacularly incompetent and debauched emperor (218–222 CE); even worse than Caligula

30-SECOND TEXT
Matthew Nicholls

Though the western empire fell in the 5th C CE, the eastern empire lasted until the Fall of Constantinople in 1453.

EMPIRE & EXPANSION

the 30-second history

In a millennium of conquest

Rome grew from a cluster of hilltop villages to be mistress of territory from Scotland to the Nile delta, Spain to Syria. Early legendary accounts suggest that as its power expanded Rome clashed with its Italic neighbors, the Latins, Sabines, and Etruscans, acquiring a local supremacy partly through conquest and partly through co-opting rivals by treaty and absorption. By the end of the fifth century BCE this process was largely complete and Rome's broadening horizons brought her into conflict with regional Italian powers and then Mediterranean rivals. The Carthaginians were defeated in the Punic Wars (third and second centuries BCE). Parts of present-day Spain, Greece, and Turkey fell to Roman arms and became tax-paying provinces. Julius Caesar subdued Gaul in the mid-first century BCE. By then, the flow of plunder into Rome and the disruptive loyalties of her armies were fracturing the republican state. The new imperial government of Augustus and his successors resumed the pattern of conquest. The empire reached its farthest limits under Trajan (ruled 98–117 CE), and its borders hardened as the momentum of conquest fizzled out. By the fifth century CE invasion, insurrection, and civil war had weakened the empire to the point of collapse.

3-SECOND SURVEY
"To spare the conquered, but to war down the proud"—this, according to the poet Virgil, was Rome's divinely inspired imperial mission.

3-MINUTE EXCAVATION
Roman commentators were not above criticizing the spread of Roman power. Writers like Tacitus enjoyed comparing hardy, martial, barbarian tribes on the frontier with the corruption and decadence of imperial Rome. Tacitus gives inspiring (but fictional) anti-Roman speeches to various barbarian chieftains, including British rebel queen Boudicca and the Scottish warlord Calgacus: the latter famously said "to plunder, slaughter, and robbery they give the false name of empire; and where they make a desert, they call it peace."

RELATED HISTORIES
See also
LIFE IN THE ROMAN PROVINCES
page 48

3-SECOND BIOGRAPHIES
SCIPIO AFRICANUS
236–183 BCE
Roman general who defeated Rome's arch-enemy Hannibal, ending the second Punic War against Carthage

JULIUS CAESAR
ca. 100–44 BCE
Roman general and politician who extended the bounds of the Roman empire by conquering Gaul

CONSTANTINE THE GREAT
272–337 CE
Rome's first Christian emperor, who divided the empire into eastern and western halves

30-SECOND TEXT
Matthew Nicholls

Rome left its imprint on many aspects of society, culture, and architecture in its vast territory in Europe, Asia, and Africa.

THE ROMAN LEGION

the 30-second history

The army of the early Roman

state was composed of citizen-soldiers who had sufficient wealth to provide their own armor, and to take time away from home to fight. As Rome expanded it needed larger and more permanent armies, capable of sustaining long, distant campaigns. The reforms of the general and politician Marius in the late second century BCE improved pay and removed the wealth qualification, creating a standing army that could be a career choice for poor citizens. This increased both the manpower and the experience of the legions, but also made them look to their individual commanders for reward—a factor partly responsible for Rome's first-century BCE civil wars. By the first century CE the legion had matured into a unit of about 5,200 legionaries, divided into ten cohorts of six centuries each. Legions swore loyalty to the emperor and had numbers and names (a proud "regimental" history). Other types of troops— light infantry, cavalry, archers—were levied as "auxiliaries" from allied states and rewarded with Roman citizenship on discharge. Battlefield tactics were complemented by high levels of discipline and training, backed by a military-minded state able to engage in complex campaigns. The result was a formidable military establishment.

3-SECOND SURVEY
The army's structures evolved into a well-drilled force of legions (28 under Augustus), composed of sub-units and assisted by auxiliary forces.

3-MINUTE EXCAVATION
The commanding officers of each legion—the legate and his prefects—tended to be men of high social status, often building a political career. The centurions, though, could be long-service professionals promoted from the ranks. From 8-man tent-teams (*contubernia*), through 80-man centuries, to 6-century cohorts, to legions, the army's structure built *esprit de corps*. As the army increasingly recruited from overseas provinces, its structure, cash pay, discipline, gods, and Latin language helped turn recruits into Romans.

RELATED HISTORIES
See also
THE ROMAN LEGIONARY
page 30

CITIZENSHIP
page 36

3-SECOND BIOGRAPHY
GAIUS MARIUS
157–86 BCE
Roman reforming general and politician

30-SECOND TEXT
Matthew Nicholls

Rome looked to the loyalty and discipline of the legions—its chief military force—to maintain control and influence throughout the empire.

THE ROMAN LEGIONARY

the 30-second history

We all have a picture of the "typical" well-equipped Roman legionary. In reality the Roman army's arms and tactics changed and adapted over almost a millennium of activity across the ancient world. One consistent factor that explains Roman success is the insistence on good discipline and drill— Roman generals and writers recognized the importance of good order both in the peacetime army and in battle. After Marius's reforms, legionary equipment and armor started to resemble a more "regular" pattern. Each man carried an iron-tipped javelin (*pila*) to hurl before closing on the enemy for combat with sword (*gladius* or *spatha*) and long rectangular or oval shield (*scutum*). The latter could be locked together with neighboring soldiers in a defensive formation such as the famous "tortoise." Legionary helmets evolved to offer neck protection and cheek, brow, and ear guards. Heavy chainmail was replaced by segmented plate armor. Made of iron straps and hoops to cover torso and shoulders and held together with leather fittings, this combined protection and flexibility. Serving for up to 25 years, legionaries enjoyed relatively good pay and status and the prospect of a land grant or cash bonus on discharge: emperors knew to keep them onside.

3-SECOND SURVEY
The arms and tactics of the Roman army's core soldiers developed over the centuries into its familiar form.

3-MINUTE EXCAVATION
"It is the gods' will that ... Rome shall be the capital of the world; therefore let them cultivate the arts of war"—Livy, writing under Augustus, expressed the common Roman understanding that the success and identity of the state was divinely ordained, and bound up in its prowess on the battlefield. For Virgil, Rome's imperial destiny was "to spare the conquered but to war down the proud." The citizen-legionary was a vital expression of this national purpose, featuring in much imperial art.

RELATED HISTORIES
See also
EMPIRE & EXPANSION
page 26

THE ROMAN LEGION
page 28

3-SECOND BIOGRAPHIES
GAIUS MARIUS
157–86 BCE
Roman reforming general and politician

TRAJAN
53–117 CE
Military commander and philanthropic emperor who left a legacy of enduring landmarks

30-SECOND TEXT
Matthew Nicholls

Military might made Rome rich as well as powerful; maintaining a standing army was key to the success and endurance of its claim to be capital of the ancient world.

PEOPLE & SOCIETY

citizens, *cives Romani* Roman citizenship was a privileged status that afforded its holder various rights and privileges including *ius commercii* (the right to enter into legal contracts and hold property) and *ius conubii* (the right to marry a Roman citizen and to pass on citizenship to children). The most privileged group, citizens *optimo iure*, also enjoyed *ius suffragii* (the right to vote in Roman assemblies) and *ius honorum* (the right to hold political office). Women and freed slaves had more limited citizen rights.

censor, census A Roman magistrate (one of a pair) elected for 18 months to maintain the list (*census*) of Roman citizens. Their authority extended to supervising the moral conduct of citizens, revising the membership of the senate, and letting public contracts. Under the principate the emperors assumed responsibility for the censors' functions.

cursus honorum The career path of an ambitious Roman senator, ascending through the various grades of magistracy (with their minimum age requirements) to the consulship and censorship.

epigraphic Term used to describe the thousands of inscriptions placed on Roman buildings and statues.

***eques* (pl. *equites*)** A social class of Roman "knights," in origin the cavalry troops of republican Rome and later the leading gentry of Italy and the provinces. Less wealthy and powerful than the political senatorial class, but influential in the military, commercial life, and the courts. Emperors used the *equites* in a variety of administrative roles.

freedmen Roman slaves could aspire to winning their freedom through manumission (literally, "sending from the hand"), bestowed by their master or left in their wills. A freedman—or woman—became a citizen, but still owed certain obligations to his or her former master, and was barred from holding public office.

governor The official who ran a province of the Roman empire—usually a former magistrate of the Roman state.

Latins Inhabitants of Latium, the area of central Italy where Rome was founded.

manumission *See* **freedmen**

new men *Novus homo* or "new man" was a term used in the late republic for the first man of a Roman family to reach the senate or consulship, penetrating the closed world of the nobility. Marius and Cicero are examples.

patrician A privileged aristocratic class of Roman citizens who had a monopoly on political office and priesthoods in the early Roman republic. During the principate, the emperors bestowed hereditary patrician status on their supporters.

paterfamilias, patria potestas The head of a Roman family, with various degrees of legal and moral authority (*patria potestas*) over wife, children, clients, slaves, and freedmen.

plebeian The non-patrician citizenry of Rome. Initially excluded from power, they won equality and political representation by 287 BCE through the "conflict of the orders," a two-century long struggle in which they threatened to leave Rome altogether if their demands were not met.

principate Name for the system of one-man rule established by Augustus, Rome's first emperor or *princeps* (a Latin word that translates roughly as "first citizen").

proscription The public outlawing of an individual and the confiscation of his property. Used by Sulla, Mark Antony, and Octavian (the future Augustus) to get rid of enemies and to raise money; widely feared and resented.

salutatio The formal morning ceremony in which Roman citizen clients visited the house of their patron to greet him and perhaps receive a favor or gift.

socii Rome's allied communities: the peoples and city-states in the Italian peninsula bound by formal agreement in treaties to provide men and monies to Rome.

tribute of the plebs Magistrate charged with defending the interests of the plebeians, and granted special powers and privileges to do so.

Vestal Virgins The six priestesses of Vesta, the Roman goddess of the hearth-fire, who were charged with certain sacred duties and forbidden marriage until their term of at least 30 years' service had ended.

CITIZENSHIP

the 30-second history

Roman citizens, the *cives Romani*, were the men who ran Rome: citizens enjoyed the right to vote and the right to stand for office, the right to sue another citizen and the right to stand trial if accused of a crime—although they were also obliged to pay tax and take up arms for their country. Yet it was their decision-making power—the opportunity to choose Rome's leaders and shape its future—that carried most weight, for the political system placed that power in the hands of the people. Individuals voted as members of a tribe, and their collective tribal vote was counted. During the Republic, full enfranchisement was restricted to men born to citizen parents within a legal marriage; women, freed slaves, and members of local Latin-speaking tribes had more limited rights. The year 90 BCE, however, marked the transformation of Roman citizen membership: Rome's Italian allies went to war to secure citizenship—and the vote—for themselves. The so-called Social War ended in 88 BCE, when the Romans passed a law granting full citizenship to both Latins and allies. However, by the turn of the century, Rome was ruled by an emperor and, although citizens still voted, it was with diminished influence. Citizenship had been fundamentally redefined.

The privileges of citizenship, which carried political and legal status, were desired by Romans and barbarians alike.

SLAVERY

the 30-second history

The Roman economy and way of life depended on the unpaid labour of slaves. Male and female slaves provided skilled and unskilled services, not just performing back-breaking work in the fields and mines, but tutoring children, balancing the books, and providing easy sources of sexual satisfaction. A rich Roman might own 500 slaves—and the number in the imperial household probably exceeded 20,000, where a slave could reach heady heights of power and influence beyond many free citizens. Slaves perhaps numbered 25 percent of Rome's population. Life as a slave could be brutal: tens of thousands were worked to death in mines and quarries. As items of property, slaves had no rights and little voice of their own. Many must have been treated no better than animals, but others were surely considered one of the family. Some were lucky enough to buy or be granted their freedom. Manumission brought citizen status, but freed slaves never quite lost their servile origins. Full citizen rights were denied to first-generation freedmen and patronage relationships ensured that owners continued to profit from them—the business ventures of experienced freedmen could be very successful, making ex-slaves number among some of the wealthiest Romans.

3-SECOND SURVEY
Roman slaves were the workforce of Rome, but they had no legal personhood—they were defined not as individuals with rights but as property, or chattels.

3-MINUTE EXCAVATION
In 73 BCE, a gang of slaves led by Spartacus escaped from a gladiatorial school in Capua. Soon their ranks swelled with more escaped slaves. Spartacus proved himself an excellent tactician and led the legions of Crassus and Pompey on a merry dance around central Italy until his army was finally defeated in 71 BCE. Six thousand captured slaves were crucified along the Appian Way, but Spartacus's body was never found.

RELATED HISTORIES
See also
CITIZENSHIP
page 36

SOCIAL CLASS & STATUS
page 40

MEN & WOMEN
page 44

3-SECOND BIOGRAPHIES
MARCUS LICINIUS CRASSUS
115–53 BCE
Roman general and politician who later entered into the political partnership with Pompey and Caesar

POMPEY THE GREAT
106–48 BCE
Enormously successful Roman general who celebrated three triumphs but was beheaded during civil war

30-SECOND TEXT
Susanne Turner

For wealthy Romans, the practice of slavery was accepted as the norm on which their privileged lifestyle depended.

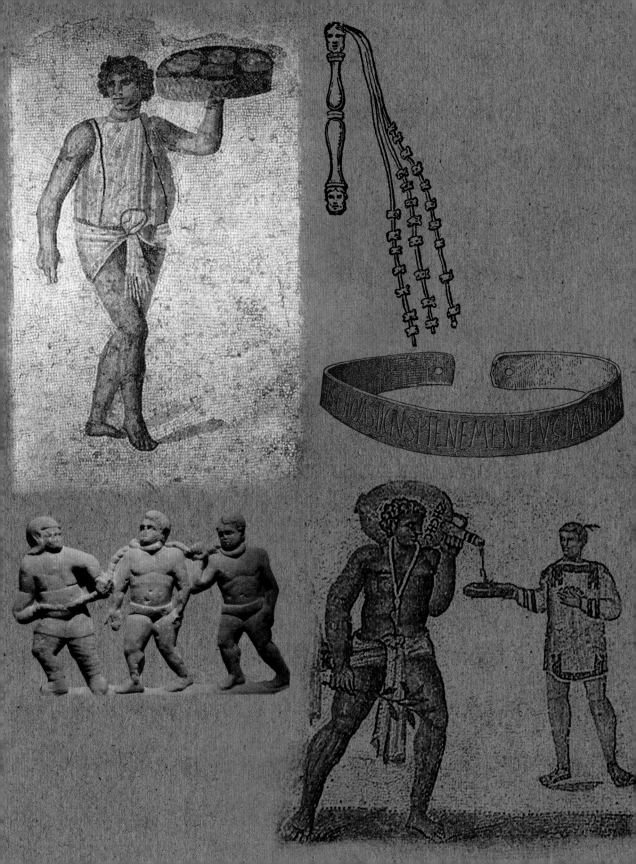

SOCIAL CLASS & STATUS

the 30-second history

3-SECOND SURVEY
Roman citizens were traditionally divided into patricians and plebeians. While the plebs were more numerous, political power was concentrated in the hands of the patricians.

3-MINUTE EXCAVATION
Marcus Tullius Cicero was a *novus homo* or "new man." His family was of the equestrian order and no members of the senate numbered among his ancestors: he had neither family name nor connections to exploit to gain his first step on the *cursus honorum*. He was no soldier, so he relied on his skill in the lawcourts. His command of words made him the first new man in 80 years to become consul, in 63 BCE.

The inhabitants of Ancient Rome were not born equal. Being a slave is sometimes described as a form of "social death" and even wealthy freedmen never shook off the stigma of their lowly origins. But not all citizens were of equal rank or influence: Roman society was hierarchical. Citizens were born either patrician or plebeian. Political and religious power was entrusted primarily to the patricians, although the position of the tribune of the plebs ensured that the latter had a political voice. The census further divided the aristocratic class into senatorial and equestrian orders by wealth: to qualify as an *eques* a man had to prove he held property valued at 400,000 sesterces; to be a senator he had to be worth 1,000,000. Movement between the orders, while not impossible, was difficult. Men who managed to progress from equestrian rank into the senate were known as "new men." Aristocratic and lesser men were, however, tied by relationships of patronage. Each morning, clients flocked to the houses of their patrons, demonstrating their loyalty in a ritual called *salutatio*. Patronage was mutually beneficial: clients gained financial and political support, patrons gained a network of loyal representatives.

RELATED HISTORIES
See also
CITIZENSHIP
page 36

SLAVERY
page 38

MEN & WOMEN
page 44

3-SECOND BIOGRAPHIES
GAIUS MARIUS
157–83 BCE
Roman general and new man, famed for reforming the Roman army

MARCUS TULLIUS CICERO
106–43 BCE
Roman orator, statesman, philosopher, and new man

30-SECOND TEXT
Susanne Turner

Class was rigidly bound, legally enforced, and reinforced by dress code; the toga was worn to denote the power and social standing of citizens.

63 BCE
Born Gaius Octavius

47 BCE
Appointed pontifex, or priest

September 13th, 45 BCE
Julius Caesar, by now supreme at Rome, names Octavius as his heir

March 15th, 44 BCE
Assassination of Caesar

43 BCE
Formation of second triumvirate between Octavian, Antony, and Lepidus

39 BCE
Octavian marries Livia Drusilla

30S BCE
Victories against foreign and domestic enemies; relationship with Antony breaks down

31 BCE
Victory over Antony at the naval battle of Actium, followed by the conquest of Egypt

27 BCE
Octavian "restores the republic" by reinstating the senate and magistrates, and takes the title Augustus

23 BCE
Second constitutional settlement, organizing Augustus's power at Rome and in the provinces

18–17 BCE
Moral and social legislation passed

14 CE
Augustus dies in his late seventies; power passes to his stepson Tiberius, the second emperor of Rome

AUGUSTUS

Augustus was Rome's first

emperor. He inherited the wreckage of the republican state and against the odds crafted it into a lasting imperial system centered on his own person. Though his methods were frequently harsh, by putting an end to civil war he ushered in an era of peace that he (and others) presented as a golden age for Rome.

Born Gaius Octavius, "Augustus" (meaning, loosely, "revered," or "sacred") was the title he took in 27 BCE. He impressed his great-uncle Julius Caesar and was adopted as his heir. When Caesar was assassinated in 44 BCE, the 17-year-old moved quickly to assume the leadership of the pro-Caesar faction. An uneasy coalition with Caesar's old partner Marc Antony disintegrated into civil war, which ended with the death of Antony and Cleopatra in 30 BCE and the Roman conquest of Egypt.

Now undisputed ruler of Rome, Augustus sought to accommodate his own personal authority within the remains of the republican constitution, to provide a semblance of reassuring continuity. In reality his continually renewed tenure of the highest offices, and complete control of appointments to the senate and other posts, gave him unprecedented power.

Augustus justified this position to his subjects partly through his cultural patronage, sponsoring a generation of poets, including Horace and Virgil, and erecting splendid public buildings across Rome (leading him to boast that he had "found Rome a city of brick and left it a city of marble"). He was also successful in war, doubling the size of the empire and fostering a sense of Rome's divinely ordained dominion.

Augustus presented himself as a fatherlike figure, and his own family as a model for the proper conduct expected of Romans through his social legislation on marriage and childbearing. Though this caused problems— Augustus had to exile his own daughter and granddaughter for their adultery— it allowed him to lay the foundations of a dynastic system. His own long life, and the inevitable chicanery of palace politics, saw several choices of successor come and go before he had to settle on his morose stepson Tiberius, but his system of individual imperial rule survived for three centuries. Like Julius Caesar, he was deified after his death by successors reliant on his legacy for their legitimacy.

Matthew Nicholls

MEN & WOMEN

the 30-second history

The traditional history of Rome

is, in so many ways, a history of men. Roman men ruled the roost, at home and away. In the public arena, it was men who went to war, who held office and priesthoods, who ruled as emperors—and who wrote history. At home, the (male) head was the *paterfamilias*, who held *patria potestas*—the power to make life and death choices for his household, as well as more pedestrian choices about family finances and worshipping ancestral gods. Children, male and female, stayed under the *patria potestas* of the *paterfamilias* for his lifetime even after they married. By the early empire, women remained under their father's *patria potestas* and husbands had no legal control over them; marriage was, in a sense, a source of empowerment and wives enjoyed a certain degree of freedom. Women could own and inherit property, write wills, and run businesses. But they were never full citizens; they had no vote and could not stand for office. Only the Vestal Virgins gained a degree of autonomy and official visibility, committed from childhood to a life of celibacy and ritual service by their patrician families. For most women, in all walks of life, opportunities remained defined by men.

RELATED HISTORIES
See also
CITIZENSHIP
page 36

SEX
page 46

3-SECOND SURVEY
Power, political and domestic, was concentrated in the hands of men, but women maintained a sometimes surprising degree of freedom.

3-MINUTE EXCAVATION
Divorce was not uncommon in the Roman world, but emperor Augustus tried to crack down on husband/ wife swapping and bachelordom, aimed at ensuring the senatorial class committed to marriage and reproduced. He passed laws rewarding the birth of multiple children and penalizing young men who failed to marry. He even made adultery punishable by banishment—and unfortunately, in 2 BCE, was forced to exile his own daughter for this crime.

3-SECOND BIOGRAPHIES
AUGUSTUS
63 BCE—14 CE
First Roman emperor, whose moral legislation made the private lives of citizens a concern of the state

JULIA THE ELDER
39 BCE—14 CE
Augustus's only daughter, died in exile on a tiny island

30-SECOND TEXT
Susanne Turner

Ancient Rome was a patriarchal society— the role and status of women were defined by those of their fathers or husbands.

SEX

the 30-second history

Sex seems to have been rife in the Roman world: emperors had multiple partners (of both sexes), poets turned their mistresses into muses, house-owners decorated their walls with erotic images (including, memorably, the god Priapus weighing his own impressive member—in an entrance hall!); even the streets were lined with disembodied penises. But it wasn't all orgies, wife-swapping, and sexual abandon: such stories are doubtless more fantasy than reality. *Pudor* (shame, modesty) was enshrined in law and the censors could—and did—expel senators for sexual misdemeanor. The real pressure to uphold sexual standards was placed on women, who were expected to exhibit proper *pudicitia* (modesty, chastity) at all times. *Pudicitia* must often have been easier for elite women to embody than for their social inferiors; a prostitute or slave who found herself sexually available to her master likely found it near impossible to control her sexual boundaries; sexual roles—for both men and women—were codified according to social status. But a word of warning: Roman sexualities don't map exactly onto ours. Romans had no words to express the identities "hetero-" or "homosexual" and seem to have been more concerned with sexual acts—who took active and passive roles—than sexual identities.

RELATED HISTORIES
See also
CITIZENSHIP
page 36

SOCIAL CLASS & STATUS
page 40

MEN & WOMEN
page 44

3-SECOND BIOGRAPHIES
MESSALINA
ca. 22–48 CE
Third wife of Claudius and a notorious nymphomaniac

ELAGABALUS
205–222 CE
Juvenile emperor (218–222 CE), known more for his sexual depravity than his reign

30-SECOND TEXT
Susanne Turner

Erotica is well-represented in ancient Roman literature and art but in reality sexual conduct was bound up with power, status, and social norms.

LIFE IN THE ROMAN PROVINCES

the 30-second history

The geographically extensive and demographically diverse Roman empire was ruled by the emperor and his provincial governors, or by pliable "client kings," and peace kept by the legions, but in reality these forces were spread thin, often concentrated at trouble points, and impeded by the slow pace of communications. Much of the Roman empire knew Rome as a relatively distant presence, coming into contact with Roman power through law, taxation, census, and coinage (as Christ's "render unto Caesar" remark shows). Roman influence could be felt in the countryside, as large villa estates and productive farming methods fed distant Roman markets, but it was particularly in the towns and cities of the empire where distinctive architectural forms suggested Roman ways of living: fora, bathhouses, theaters, and amphitheaters set in straight grids of streets. The extent to which we can call this "Romanization" is still hotly debated, however; Rome rarely rode roughshod over local cultures, tending more to co-opt and reward willing indigenous factions. The successful elites—the men who wrote our literary and epigraphic sources—responded with enthusiasm, leading the adoption of Roman styles of living, but with many rich local variations; resistance and discontent are naturally harder to find in the surviving evidence.

3-SECOND SURVEY
Life in the provinces of the Roman empire varied dramatically according to time and place; Rome's influence was sometimes overwhelming, and sometimes subtle.

3-MINUTE EXCAVATION
Though our evidence is incomplete and differs by period and locale, it is hard to escape the conclusion that the "pax Romana" enabled an enormous upsurge in productivity and trade, and accordingly in fine architecture and the amenities of civilized living, in the provinces. Regions like Gaul or Britain that initially resisted Roman invasion produced over time some of the richest expressions of Roman provincial life, but it is difficult to know how far into society these benefits of the Roman peace extended.

RELATED HISTORIES
See also
IMPERIAL GOVERNMENT
page 24

EMPIRE & EXPANSION
page 26

TRADE & INDUSTRY
page 58

3-SECOND BIOGRAPHIES
AELIUS ARISTIDES
117–181 CE
Greek showpiece orator who lavishes praise on imperial Rome

BOUDICCA
61 CE
Iconic queen of the Iceni tribe who rose in doomed revolt, abused by Roman colonists

PLINY THE YOUNGER
61–112 CE
Roman governor of Bithynia-Pontus province (109–111); his letters tell of provincial life

30-SECOND TEXT
Matthew Nicholls

Architectural remains may skew our view that the provinces were fully "Romanized."

ROMAN LAW

the 30-second history

The rule of law was a vital part

of the spread and legacy of Roman power. Essential for articulating the activities of government and for mediating social and commercial relationships, Rome's formidable legal tradition provided a common framework in an increasingly large and disparate empire. Rome had been governed by written laws since the earliest times: the Lapis Niger ("black stone") found in the Roman forum contains a sacred law code from as early as the sixth century BCE. As the state transformed into a republic and acquired its first overseas territories, its need for clear and consistent laws, and magistrates, increased; the arrival of the emperors added another layer. From the "Twelve Tables" of ca. 450 BCE to Justinian's sixth-century CE legal codification, Rome built up a thousand years of civil, magisterial, and imperial law. Political power in the Roman state was often won through excellence as a courtroom lawyer; the jobs of many Roman politicians, among them provincial governors, included deciding cases as magistrates. In the late republic and empire, learned "jurists" assisted the emperor and his magistrates with legal opinions, edicts, and commentaries, analyzing and modifying the ever-growing body of laws to ensure universality and consistency.

RELATED HISTORIES
See also
REPUBLICAN GOVERNMENT
page 20

IMPERIAL GOVERNMENT
page 24

3-SECOND SURVEY
Though not as visible as an aqueduct or an amphitheater, Roman law was as essential to the fabric and longevity of the empire.

3-MINUTE EXCAVATION
"Justice is the constant and perpetual will to render to every man his due": so wrote Ulpian. Such learned jurists, often advisers to the emperors, established law as a profession through writing and teaching, and in doing so helped embed it deeply into Roman society. The influence of Roman law lived on in the eastern Byzantine empire and the nation-states of Europe—and, moreover, continues to do so in the Roman law courses taken by many students today.

3-SECOND BIOGRAPHIES
ULPIAN
170–228 CE
Roman jurist who advised emperors of the early third century CE

JUSTINIAN I
ca. 482–565 CE
Byzantine Roman emperor (527–565 CE)

30-SECOND TEXT
Matthew Nicholls

Law and the principle of justice are among Rome's greatest achievements, which served the republic and empire, and continued into European legal systems of the Middle Ages and beyond.

ROMAN LIFE

de Agri cultura The oldest surviving work of Latin prose, a treatise on agriculture by Cato the Elder. Written in ca. 160 BCE, it sets out how to make money from a slave-run, villa estate.

amphitheater A purpose-built elliptical arena for gladiatorial combat and other entertainment events. Not to be confused with theater.

amphora A large pottery vessel used for transporting wine, oil, and other goods. Amphorae are a vital source of evidence for ancient trading patterns.

annona A handout of grain to citizens living in Rome, initially subsidized and then free—a vital part of the "bread and circuses" handed out by emperors.

"bread and circuses" *Panem et circenses*, a cynical phrase coined by second-century CE satirist Juvenal to signify the emperors' generosity toward the urban population of Rome through the provision of cheap food and free entertainment.

consul The top magistrate of the Roman republic; each year two were elected, to keep each other in check.

Dacia An eastern Roman province in what is now Romania, finally conquered by Trajan. An important source of metal ore.

denarius (**pl.** *denarii*) The most important silver denomination of Roman coinage: a basic unit of currency.

dietetics The careful prescription of diet and lifestyle to restore or preserve health.

garum A fish sauce loved by the Romans, made from salted, fermented fish intestines. An important commodity manufactured and traded throughout the empire, adding an intense salty savor to dishes (the nearest seasoning equivalent today is perhaps a Thai fish sauce). By-products, such as the pungent paste *allec*, were also used as condiments.

Gaul An area of Roman imperial rule covering present-day France, western Switzerland, northern Italy, Belgium, Luxembourg, and western Germany. Its conquest was completed by Julius Caesar in the 50s BCE. The region was divided into several Roman provinces and remained within the empire until its final dissolution centuries later.

governor The official who ran a province of the Roman empire—usually the position was held by a former magistrate of the Roman state, such as a consul.

Iberia The peninsula containing modern Spain and Portugal was conquered by Rome during the Punic Wars and divided into the various provinces of Roman Hispania from 197 BCE.

obelisk A tall, tapering, four-sided monument carved by the ancient Egyptians out of granite; many were brought to Rome as impressive trophies of conquest.

oleoculture The cultivation of olives to press for oil.

orthogonal Grid-like—a typical Roman way of dividing up land for fields or city streets.

panegyric A formal, setpiece speech containing praise.

pantomime A highly popular Roman form of theater entertainment, involving words, gestures, song, and dance.

Punic Wars A series of three bitter wars between Rome and Carthage (a powerful rival state on the coast of North Africa), fought in the third and second centuries BCE, culminating with the fall and sack of Carthage in 146 BCE.

sestertius **(pl. *sestertii*)** A common base-metal Roman coin, worth a quarter of a silver *denarius* (roughly a day's wage) or 1 percent of a gold *aureus*.

tetrarchy The modern name for the college of four emperors introduced by Diocletian in 293 CE (one senior "Augustus" and one junior "Caesar" in each half of the empire, which was divided into east and west).

theater A semicircular building with stage and seating, for plays and pantomimes. Not to be confused with amphitheater.

tribune of the plebs An elected official of the Roman state, traditionally charged with protecting the interests of the common people (plebeians).

De Medicina An eight-book Latin treatise on medicine, originally part of a larger encyclopedia written in the first century CE by Aulus Cornelius Celsus.

viticulture The cultivation of grape vines for wine.

AGRICULTURE

the 30-second history

3-SECOND SURVEY
When Rome destroyed Carthage in 146 BCE Mago's agricultural treatise was the only expression of Carthaginian culture that the Roman senate deemed worth saving.

3-MINUTE EXCAVATION
Many parts of the Roman countryside were intensively settled and farmed. Farms and villas dotted the landscape and the Roman field system, characterized by orthogonal grids creating regular plots, still survives in the modern landscape in some regions. Whereas in the Republican period Italy exported wine—an amphora of wine would be traded for a slave among Celtic tribes—later, large quantities of grain, wine, and oil were imported into Rome to sustain her one million inhabitants.

Agriculture played a fundamental role in the Roman world. In both the republic and empire alike, social standing and political organization were based on landed wealth and many members of the elite took a direct interest in how best to manage their estates and which crops to grow; some even wrote treatises on agriculture. The main cash crops were grain, grapes, and olives (the "Mediterranean triad"). A larger portion of Italy was brought under cultivation in Roman times than in later ages and in regions such as Puglia modern-day olive trees may be the descendants of trees planted by the Romans. Elsewhere in the empire Roman settlers brought with them intensive viticulture and oleoculture; within a few generations, these regions (for example Gaul and Hispania) were exporting their wine and oil widely. Engineering projects, including extensive irrigation works, brought inhospitable regions, such as large portions of pre-desert North Africa, under cultivation. It is often assumed that antiquity was characterized by technological stagnation, but archaeological research has shown that innovations relating to irrigation, including the Archimedean screw, and to agricultural processing (grain and water-powered mills and wine and oil presses) were introduced to many parts of the Roman empire.

RELATED HISTORIES
See also
REPUBLICAN GOVERNMENT
page 20

CITIZENSHIP
page 36

SOCIAL CLASS & STATUS
page 40

TRADE & INDUSTRY
page 58

3-SECOND BIOGRAPHIES
LUCIUS QUINCTIUS CINCINNATUS
519–430 BCE
Statesman and figure of early Rome; he was plowing his modest plot when called upon to defend Rome as military dictator

MARCUS PORCIUS CATO
234–149 BCE
Statesman and author of the earliest Latin treatise on agriculture (de Agri cultura), which survives in its entirety

30-SECOND TEXT
Annalisa Marzano

Under the Romans, farming practice shifted from substistence to demand-led production.

TRADE & INDUSTRY

the 30-second history

Trade played an important role in the Roman world; many extraction and manufacturing activities, from quarrying, mining, pottery, and glass-making to food-processing and textiles, were connected with trade. Roman towns had shops and workshops: sometimes entire streets specialized in the manufacture and sale of specific items. Pottery and salted fish are interesting examples of large-scale production and trade. From the first century BCE, Arretine tableware (from ancient Arezzo, Tuscany) was very popular in the Roman world, with branch workshops established outside of Italy. At La Graufesenque (France), collaboration among workshops allowed for impressive results; the 24-acre (10-ha) settlement had 50 kilns and some 200 workers, producing one million items per season. The production of the fish sauces (*garum, allec*) used as seasoning in Roman cuisine took place at many coastal sites, often on a large scale. Fish-salting factories with batteries of masonry salting vats were present in southern Spain, North Africa, Sicily, Normandy, and around the Black Sea. Their produce, packed in amphorae, was exported throughout the empire as far as Hadrian's Wall in the north and the Garamantian settlements in the Saharan south (modern Libya).

3-SECOND SURVEY
Throughout the Roman world standardization and division of labor improved both production and distribution in many sectors.

3-MINUTE EXCAVATION
Long-distance trade contributed to state revenues because of a 25 percent custom tax across the empire's frontiers and a 5 percent tax across provincial boundaries. Such trade levies could add considerably to the state coffers, given that, according to Strabo, every year 120 ships sailed to India from the Red Sea and surviving documentary sources show that enormously valuable cargoes, each worth millions of sesterces, could be carried.

RELATED HISTORIES
See also
SLAVERY
page 38

AGRICULTURE
page 56

COINAGE & CURRENCY
page 60

3-SECOND BIOGRAPHIES
DOMITIAN
51–96 CE
Emperor (81–96 CE) who passed legislation to reduce the number of vineyards in the provinces, possibly to favor the export of Italian wine

AULUS UMBRICIUS SCAURUS
fl. 60s/70s CE
Pompeian businessman running a successful *garum*-manufacturing business in Pompeii, whose products were widely exported

30-SECOND TEXT
Annalisa Marzano

Archaeological finds indicate that goods were traded across huge distances in the empire and beyond.

COINAGE & CURRENCY

the 30-second history

Until the early third century BCE

Rome made official payments using uncoined masses of bronze (*aes rude*) and cast bronze ingots (*aes signatum*). When Rome started to mint coins it took as model the coinage of the nearby Greek city of Neapolis (Naples) and used its mint. By 211 BCE Rome had its own mint and coined silver *denarii*, which for centuries remained the most important denomination of the Roman monetary system, and smaller bronze denominations. Later, Augustus introduced a gold coin (*aureus*), whose value was linked to the *denarius*. However, the Greek world kept its monetary system based on the silver drachm rather than the *denarius* and provincial mints continued to issue their own bronze coins for local circulation; every major city had money exchangers able to convert different currencies. During the third century CE the weight and metal content of Roman coins diminished sharply, until Constantine reformed the monetary system by introducing the gold *solidus*. The quality and metal content of early imperial *aurei* and *denarii* meant they were widely appreciated as means of exchange: hoards of Roman coins have been found in India, fruit of the long-distance trade that brought to the Mediterranean spices and pearls.

3-SECOND SURVEY
The Latin word for bronze, *aes*, was the colloquial word for money, showing that bronze always remained important within the Roman monetary system.

3-MINUTE EXCAVATION
Besides being a means for commercial exchanges, Roman coins, with their images and legends, played an important role in spreading messages to the people: publicizing military victories, imperial building projects, or popularizing the image of the ruling emperor. Julius Caesar was the first to use his own portrait on coins instead of that of one of his ancestors, as had previously been customary.

RELATED HISTORY
See also
TRADE & INDUSTRY
page 58

3-SECOND BIOGRAPHIES
IUNO MONETA
Goddess; the Roman mint in her temple gives us the words "money" and "mint"

CARACALLA
188–217 CE
Emperor who devalued the *denarius* strongly and introduced the *antoninianus*, with the nominal value of two *denarii*

DIOCLETIAN
244–311 CE
Emperor, creator of the tetrarchy, who reformed the monetary system, introducing two new coins, the silver *argenteus* and the bronze *follis*

30-SECOND TEXT
Annalisa Marzano

Several Roman military conquests were driven by the need to control key sources of ore required for coinage.

EATING & DRINKING

the 30-second history

Romans took three meals a day,
but the nature of these varied depending on an individual's wealth. Eating and drinking marked religious ceremonies and public distributions of food paid for by prominent citizens. Rome even had its state-sponsored system of distribution of grain (*annona*). Eating, whether at private or public banquets, had an important social function; such dinners could be extended and elaborate affairs, serving "all the products of land and sea, rivers and air." The wealthier the person the more he tried to impress by serving guests a large selection of costly and rare foods or by having everyday foods prepared in unusual ways. Banquets were also the occasion to reinforce social hierarchy by serving different-quality foods and wines according to the guests' social standing. Ordinary Romans, however, relied on taverns and street vendors for cooked food, since many urban dwellings were without kitchens. Staples were olive oil, wine, and cereals consumed either as bread or porridge, supplemented by pulses, vegetables, cheese, eggs, and, occasionally, meat and fish, although in coastal settlements options were greater: excavations at Herculaneum, a city destroyed (like Pompeii) by Vesuvius in 79 CE, revealed that inhabitants enjoyed various forms of seafood.

RELATED HISTORIES
See also
SOCIAL CLASS & STATUS
page 40

AGRICULTURE
page 56

TRADE & INDUSTRY
page 58

3-SECOND BIOGRAPHIES
L. LICINIUS LUCULLUS
1st century BCE
Roman general famous for his lavish banquets from whose name derives the English adjective Lucullan

NERO
37–68 CE
Roman emperor who passed legislation restricting inns and taverns to sell only boiled vegetables

30-SECOND TEXT
Annalisa Marzano

The wealthy Roman's diet can be inferred from archaeology, art, and a cookbook believed have been written by Caelius Apicus in the third or fourth century CE.

3-SECOND SURVEY
While eating and drinking in ancient Rome conjure an image of lavish banquets and orgies, many city-dwellers did not have the means to cook at home.

3-MINUTE EXCAVATION
Imperial Rome's food supply was politically crucial (hungry people tend to revolt). From the time of the republic, politicians had instituted monthly distribution of grain (*annona*), in order to win votes; as such, the distributions never went to the poorest people. Later, wine and salted pork were added. The state also subsidized the shipment of olive oil from abroad as testified by Monte Testaccio, an artificial hill in Rome 110 feet (33 m) high, made entirely from discarded oil amphorae.

IVNIVS

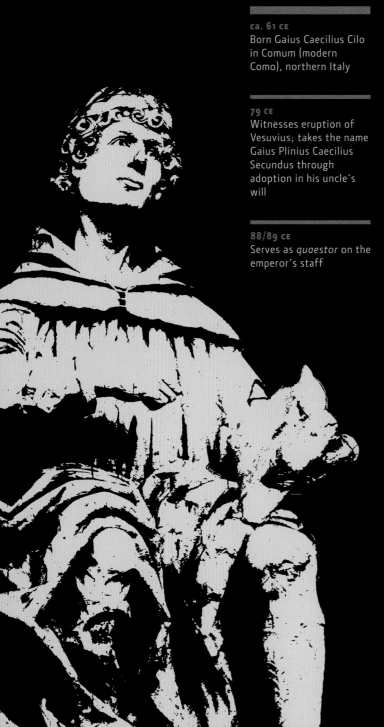

ca. 61 CE
Born Gaius Caecilius Cilo in Comum (modern Como), northern Italy

79 CE
Witnesses eruption of Vesuvius; takes the name Gaius Plinius Caecilius Secundus through adoption in his uncle's will

88/89 CE
Serves as *quaestor* on the emperor's staff

91 CE
Serves as tribune of the plebians

93 CE
Serves as *praetor*

100 CE
Consul from September to October; delivers panegyric on the emperor Trajan

110 CE
Appointed governor of the province of Bithynia-Pontus by the emperor Trajan

1471
First printed edition of Pliny's letters published in Venice

c. 1500
Fra Giovanni Giocondo discovers a manuscript containing the tenth book of Pliny's letters (correspondence with Trajan) in Paris

PLINY THE YOUNGER

The physical remains of Roman civilization can tell us a great deal about everyday life in ancient Rome, but they are not our only record of how people lived; sometimes their testimony can be supplemented by information contained in literary sources of the period. Particularly valuable in this respect are the letters of Pliny the Younger, whose correspondence sheds fascinating light on life in Rome and its provinces at the turn of the second century CE. Born during the reign of Nero, Pliny studied with the famous orator Quintilian and progressed through the conventional stages of an aristocratic Roman political career, becoming consul in 100 CE. He was later appointed governor of Bithynia-Pontus by the emperor Trajan, and the final book of his letters contains Pliny's correspondence with the emperor on administrative matters concerning his province, including consultation on the appropriate methods for dealing with a troublesome new sect—the Christians.

In addition to many details of Roman life, business, and manners at the time (including chariot racing, literary recitation, and the treatment of slaves), Pliny's letters preserve the fullest account we have of the eruption of Mount Vesuvius that destroyed the towns of Pompeii and Herculaneum in 79 CE. Pliny himself was an eyewitness to this catastrophe, in which his uncle, the writer Pliny the Elder, died, and in two letters to the historian Tacitus he gives a dramatic description of the different phases of the eruption and of the panic as those caught in the disaster attempted to escape the suffocating cloud of volcanic ash. We also learn much about Pliny's properties, about the site and layout of his villas, and about the legal cases in which he was involved; and there are touching declarations of affection from the author to his absent wife.

For all their value as a source for political and social history, Pliny's letters are by no means a purely objective record of their author's life and times; the letters were written for publication, and the writer is concerned to project an image of himself as a conscientious administrator, a cultured and versatile man of letters, and a devoted and sympathetic friend. This carefully orchestrated self-presentation is also valuable to the historian, however, since it provides important evidence for the attitudes, values, and expectations prevalent among the senatorial class at this time.

Luke Houghton

TIME & CALENDAR

the 30-second history

The Roman year (which began in March until 153 BCE, when January became the first month) was governed by calendars marking days suitable and unsuitable for public business, religious festivals, and other events. There was also an eight-day weekly cycle, marked A to H in inscribed public calendars. Over the years, this civic calendar got badly out of step with the natural solar year. Julius Caesar remedied this by making the year 46 BCE 445 days long and then imposing the Julian calendar, which was based on sound astronomical calculation and is still used by the Orthodox churches. The Romans, like the Greeks, dated events by magistrates' years of office, in their case the consuls. An absolute numerical date could also be given in years from the foundation of the city of Rome, traditionally held to be 753 BCE. For telling the time, night and day were each divided into 12 equal hours. Since daylight varies by date and latitude, hours were not the same length from season to season or in different places, but this did not greatly matter—a relative measure of time was good enough for most practical purposes, and sundials were reliable timepieces in the sunny Mediterranean.

To reinforce the idea that Augustus's rule was supported by the heavenly cycle, the months of Quintilis and Sextilis were changed to "July" and "August" (derived from Julius and Augustus.)

H X
N
A VIIII VIN
B VII
C VII ROB N
D VII

ORBITE D'URANUS

URANUS

ORBITE DE SATURNE

ORBITE DE JUPITER

ASTEROIDES
MARS   la TERRE
        MERCURE
        VENUS
ORBITE MOYENNE

JUPITER

ENTERTAINMENT & SPORT

the 30-second history

Gladiatorial combat in the Colosseum is one of the defining images of ancient Rome. Romans certainly loved large public entertainments, though not all involved the spilling of blood. Games of all sorts evolved gradually from entertainments put on by candidates for political office (and, in the case of gladiatorial games, ritual funeral combats) into enormously elaborate and expensive displays of largesse whose success could make or break an emperor's reputation. All manner of theater shows—tragedy, comedy, mimes, dances, recitals—took place in semi-circular theaters, constructed first of wood and later of stone. Athletic contests, adopted from the Greek world, included boxing, wrestling, and the Roman favorite, chariot-racing—any open ground would do, but a purpose-built circus displayed a city's wealth and sophistication. Combat spectacles, in public squares and then in special elliptical amphitheaters, were particularly popular in Italy and the western empire and included gladiatorial combat between distinctive types of fighter. Trained and armed at considerable expense, successful gladiators could amass fame and fortune, while by some accounts one chariot racer, Diocles, was the highest-paid sportsman in human history.

3-SECOND SURVEY
Cities throughout the Roman empire hosted public entertainments on a grand scale, from pantomime to gladiatorial combat and public executions.

3-MINUTE EXCAVATION
Public spectacles, as they evolved in complexity and scale, came to be reflections of the whole Roman world in miniature. The splendid architecture, links to the politics of "bread and circuses," rules governing who was allowed to sit where, and punishment of criminals, all made a day at the games an experience that would remind the spectator of his place in the Roman world even as it entertained him.

RELATED HISTORIES
See also
CITIZENSHIP
page 36

SLAVERY
page 38

THE COLOSSEUM & CIRCUS MAXIMUS
page 118

3-SECOND BIOGRAPHIES
PRISCUS & VERUS
fl. first century CE
First gladiators to fight in the Colosseum

GAIUS APPIUS DIOCLES
ca. 130–210 CE
Roman Spaniard who amassed an incredible fortune as a successful chariot racer

30-SECOND TEXT
Matthew Nicholls

Combat was only one event in the arena of death; beast hunts and criminal executions, sometimes through the enforced enactment of mythical tales, were other entertainments.

MEDICINE

the 30-second history

Ancient medicine was part of a wide variety of therapeutic options, ranging from rational, proto-scientific treatment by doctors, and practical assistance from surgeons and midwives, through to amulets, spells, and folk remedies. Much of this leaves little trace; our understanding of ancient medicine depends on archaeological finds and surviving literary records. As in so many fields, Rome took much of its medical learning from Greece; the scientific method of Aristotle and the body of work ascribed to the Greek doctor Hippocrates, with its four bodily 'humors' (blood, phlegm, and yellow and black bile), were especially influential. Roman doctors learned from this tradition and added to it. Celsus wrote on the division of medicine into lifestyle ("dietetics"), pharmacology, and surgery. Galen, a Greek who came to Rome as physician to the emperors, left an enormous body of writings (of which some three million words survive) on anatomy, medical methods, physiology, and pharmacology, which was enormously influential throughout the history of western medicine. Archaeological finds fill out the picture. Portable medical kits containing bronze surgical instruments, ranging from simple scalpels to forceps, drills, catheters, and specula, suggest a high degree of skill. There were no anaesthetics.

RELATED HISTORIES
See also
SEX
page 46

EATING & DRINKING
page 62

3-SECOND BIOGRAPHIES
[AULUS] CORNELIUS CELSUS
fl. first century CE
Author of a key medical history
De Medicina

GALEN OF PERGAMUM
ca. 130–210 CE
Greek physician and surgeon who brought the practices of Hippocrates and others to Rome

30-SECOND TEXT
Matthew Nicholls

3-SECOND SURVEY
Roman doctors built on the different schools of Greek medical knowledge, using diet, drugs, and surgery.

3-MINUTE EXCAVATION
There was no universal training for doctors, or recognized system of qualifications. Rival schools of thought competed for reputation and business, and doctors had an intellectual grounding in what we would regard as non-medical disciplines. Galen started off as a gladiator physician (a good training in practical anatomy and surgery); he excelled as a doctor and researcher, dissecting animals and often proceeding by experiment and logic. However, he was also trained in rhetoric and philosophy and wrote several works on language, grammar, and literature.

Though ancient doctors had some scientific knowledge and therapeutic ability, prayer, sacrifice, and offerings to the gods remained important for those hoping for a cure.

LANGUAGE & LITERATURE

LANGUAGE & LITERATURE
GLOSSARY

annals Bare yearly records of civic and priestly bodies at Rome, that evolved over time into more complete historical accounts.

book Books in the Roman world were usually scrolls made of glued sheets of paper-like papyrus (the stem of an Egyptian marsh plant), wound round a central boss. The text was written in ink in columns running down the short length of the scroll, which the reader would unroll. Books in the sewn-leaf "codex" format that we use today were not unknown in the Roman world, but tended to be used for note-taking or as novelties, only taking off with the spread of the Bible. One Roman-style book might hold about 1,500 lines of writing, enough for a single Greek play or a couple of books of Homer or Virgil.

controversia A rhetorical exercise in which a student argued one or both sides in an imaginary legal case.

cursive script An everyday form of handwriting in the Roman world, often found in graffiti and on wax tablets.

epic A genre of ancient poetry, telling of heroic deeds in long works composed of lines in a distinctive poetic meter.

Etruscan(s) A neighboring civilization to Rome, from whom the Romans took many cultural, civic, and religious practices.

grammaticus A professional teacher of language, grammar, and literature to Roman boys of the upper classes in the early stages of their education.

lyric A genre of first Greek and then Latin poetry; composed in a variety of meters, lyric poems dwell on personal subjects such as love and loss.

Metamorphoses Ovid's popular 15-book poem about transformations in Roman and Greek mythology, covering more than 200 stories.

meter The repeating pattern of long and short syllables that gives different genres of Latin poetry their particular style and sound.

Natural History Huge Latin encyclopedia written by the Elder Pliny in the 70s CE. It covers many fields of knowledge, from art to zoology to technology.

Odes Four-book collection of lyric poems on Rome, life, and love by Horace, a poet active under the first emperor Augustus.

paedagogus A slave "governor" who supervised the children of a rich household, beginning their basic literacy teaching.

rhetor A teacher of rhetoric to Roman boys around the age of 15 years and older.

Sibylline Oracles A collection of prophecies in Greek verse supposedly spoken by a Sibyl (prophetess) and collected by the last king of Rome. Preserved (and renewed) through the ages, these oracles were consulted at times of national crisis.

suasoria A rhetorical exercise in which a student made a speech of advice to a historical or mythical/literary figure.

sententiae (sing. sententia) A *sententia* was the final judgment in a civil trial; the word in its plural form, *sententiae*, also came to mean a brief and pithy quotable saying.

Satyrica A picaresque, novel-like work of fiction by first-century CE author Petronius; describes the (mis)adventures of the hero Encolpius including his terrible evening at dinner with boorish millionaire Trimalchio.

The Twelve Tables An important set of written statutes from the early republic (mid-fifth century BCE), ending the patricians' legal monopoly and starting the development of Roman law.

theater A semicircular building with stage and seating, for plays and pantomimes.

toga The official dress of a Roman citizen, worn by courtroom orators and those on other forms of civic business: made from a length of woollen cloth wound around the body in a particular way.

vernacular The everyday language of common speech.

wax tablets Wooden writing tablets inlaid with wax and tied together into pairs or bundles were a popular, erasable writing surface for low-status lists, letters, contracts, and exercises. More prestigious literary writing was done on scrolls of paper-like papyrus.

LATIN

the 30-second history

The language most commonly associated with the Romans and the Roman Empire is Latin. It was, however, only one of many in the Roman empire, used alongside many other vernacular languages and dialects, often in bi- or even multilingual settings. Latin is an Indo-European language, belonging to the Latino-Faliscan branch of the Italic languages. The very term "Latin" refers to the Latini, the inhabitants of Latium, the area around Rome. Following the Roman expansion, Latin became the most common language of the Italian peninsula (and eventually of the western hemisphere of the Roman world). Whereas Latin, as it was written during the "classical age" of the first century BCE, remained in common, if fossilized, use for high literature and official communication, documentary evidence from all over the empire (private letters, graffiti, or other, non-official, inscriptions) show just how far the linguistic reality moved on. This development gave rise to the Romance languages, via spoken, or "vulgar" Latin, as its legitimate offspring. Latin has long remained the common language in academia, and, in an unbroken tradition throughout the Middle Ages and the Early modern period, continues to play a role in the Roman Catholic church.

3-SECOND SURVEY
Latin, one of many languages originally spoken in mainland Italy, became one of the most widespread languages in the world and sired the Romance languages.

3-MINUTE EXCAVATION
Despite a broad, well-evidenced tradition, our knowledge of the minutiae of the Latin language is patchy. There is also no reliable evidence for spoken as opposed to written Latin at large (including its sound), or for how the two were different from one another. The surviving remains of Latin give a distorted image; discoveries of new texts excite not only ancient historians but historians of the Latin language.

RELATED HISTORIES
See also
EDUCATION & LITERACY
page 78

RHETORIC
page 82

INSCRIPTIONS & GRAFFITI
page 90

3-SECOND BIOGRAPHIES
LIVIUS ANDRONICUS
283–200 BCE
The first named author to write in Latin and the alleged founding father of Roman drama

VARRO
116–27 BCE
Roman historian of the Latin language

MARCUS TULLIUS CICERO
106–43 BCE
Exponent, like Julius Caesar, of ideal classical Latin

30-SECOND TEXT
Peter Kruschwitz

Latin text still holds primacy of place in academia, medicine, taxonomy, law, and the church liturgy.

EDUCATION & LITERACY

the 30-second history

Roman education was primarily domestic, never regional or national. Under ongoing Greek influence, direct paternal supervision gradually incorporated professional teachers. Although a modified Greek alphabet was adopted in the seventh century BCE, for three centuries critical texts—priestly annals, "The Twelve Tables" (law code), and the "Sibylline Oracles"—remained sacred and state-owned. Colonial and military expansion from the third century BCE made writing logistically important, and scholarship began to define status. Private Greek tutors appeared: the *paedagogus* taught character and basic literacy, then the *grammaticus* literature and grammar; the *rhetor* taught declamation. Latin literature flourished as (bilingual) elite literacy spread. Documentation became the empire's lifeblood, particularly from the late republic onward: legions and provinces were managed through bulletins, financial records, and censuses; Cato's manual for landowners assumes literacy among supervisor slaves; soldiers used memoranda; senatorial decrees were publicly displayed in Rome; tombstones and monuments bore inscriptions; painted signs and graffiti covered every town. Schooling was rare, but the best-preserved evidence (from Egypt) shows an expectation that anyone could find relatives or acquaintances to write for them.

3-SECOND SURVEY
Roman education, especially literacy, was the gateway to political or military rank but involved ongoing expense, thereby reinforcing social and economic distinctions.

3-MINUTE EXCAVATION
Most writing was done on a beeswax tablet using a pointed stylus; the flattened end erased mistakes. Learning was by memorization, corporal punishment routine. Horace thanks his father for moving him to Rome to learn from a respected *grammaticus*, Orbilius, whom he calls "thrasher" (*plagosus*). Recent calculations put peak literacy below 30 percent in Italy, 10 percent in Western provinces; for women, much lower. But given the prevalence of written texts, functional "reading" was probably the norm.

RELATED HISTORY
See also
RHETORIC
page 82

3-SECOND BIOGRAPHIES
CATO THE ELDER
234–149 BCE
Conservative statesman and agricultural writer

HORACE
65–8 BCE
Poet of the Augustan period

30-SECOND TEXT
Dunstan Lowe

Roman education began around the age of seven. Female pupils ceased education aged 12, males in their late teens, sometimes capping their education by visits to world-famous lecturers, especially in Athens.

MAGRIPPALFCOSTERTIVMFECI

DRAMA

the 30-second history

Impressive ruins of Roman theater buildings have been discovered throughout the Roman empire. The city of Rome itself, however, did not get to enjoy a permanent theater building until the opening of the Theater of Pompey in the first century BCE. This late arrival shows the tension between the Roman nobility's desire to impress the people with lavish (if makeshift) structures, and the Romans' appreciation of the political nature of dramatic performances. Amassing vast numbers of the populace at a festival and then surrendering control to a playwright and a troupe of performers is a dangerous move. Rome's great comedians, Plautus and Terence, represent members of the lower classes, and their plays challenged Rome's aristocratic, male-dominated society. Plautus's slapstick humor and Terence's invention of comedic suspense and the obligatory double-plot transformed European drama. Tragedy, too, had its place on the Roman stage. However, Rome's most famous tragedian, Nero's teacher Seneca, may not have seen any of his plays performed in one of the grandiose theaters; perhaps they were too complex to stage or too subversive in nature. Of course, there was also lighthearted entertainment: mimes offered the equivalent of modern-day stand-up performances.

RELATED HISTORIES
See also
PROSE WRITING
page 86

POETRY
page 88

3-SECOND SURVEY
The Greeks may have invented drama, but the Romans perfected it: dramatic suspense, double plots, and tragic pathos are all Roman innovations.

3-MINUTE EXCAVATION
Drama is a Greek word, meaning "action." The Romans called their plays *fabulae*, meaning "stories." Several English words are related to Roman theatrical terms, which in turn originated in neighboring cultures. This includes "person" (*persona*, the character of a play, most likely of Etruscan origin), "scene" (*scaena*, the stage, originally from Greek *skene*, "tent," a place for the actors to change their costumes), and "histrionic" (*histrio*, the actor, originally from Etruscan *ister*).

3-SECOND BIOGRAPHIES
PLAUTUS
254–184 BCE
Roman comic playwright

TERENCE
195–159 BCE
Roman comic playwright, who fundamentally influenced later playwrights, including Shakespeare and Molière

SENECA
4 BCE–65 CE
Roman Stoic philosopher, statesman, adviser to the young Emperor Nero, and tragic playwright

30-SECOND TEXT
Peter Kruschwitz

Theater was part of Roman life. Plays were staged during many of the 200 religious festivals celebrated annually.

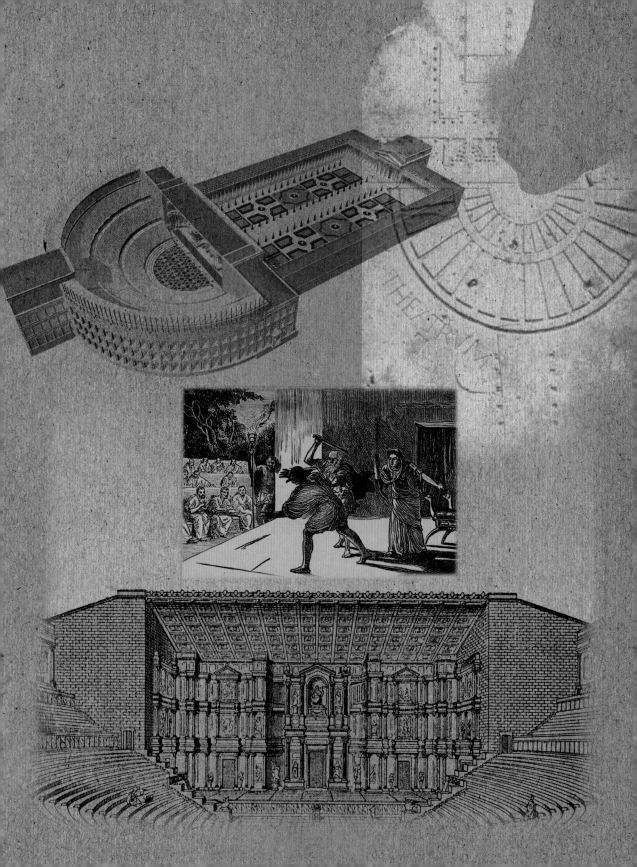

RHETORIC

the 30-second history

Rhetoric, a Greek word and
concept, became essential intellectual training
for the Roman elite. The *rhetor* was a technician
who used formal exercises to display his skill and
to train pupils. This style of education first
emerged in the fifth century BCE, when
renowned Greek debaters such as Gorgias and
Antiphon used logic and semantics as tools of
persuasion. Aspects of performance, including
gestures and intonation, were also carefully
scrutinized. Romans valued public speaking too;
during the third and second centuries BCE, they
imported rhetoricians among other Greek cultural
prizes. Two styles of practice speech that were
already evolving became standard at Rome. The
suasoria, resembling philosophical or political
debates, offers advice to a mythical or historical
character. Should Agamemnon sacrifice his
daughter? Should Cicero burn his writings to save
his life? The more challenging *controversia* is a
role-playing speech, tackling a complex case
involving imaginary laws. For example, a law
requires female rape victims to choose between
marrying the attacker without dowry, or
executing him. Someone rapes two girls, and the
victims choose differently. Should he be married
or executed? Such rigorous exercises and
techniques, including *sententiae*—quotable,
proverb-like maxims—influenced how elite
authors and poets wrote.

3-SECOND SURVEY
During the Republic,
well-composed and
well-performed speeches
decided the nation's fate.
However, after the
emperors absorbed the
Senate's authority, rhetoric
was mainly valued as
an artform.

3-MINUTE EXCAVATION
Ancient Roman discussions
of declamation stress
the importance of body
language. Orators (unlike
actors) were of high social
standing, and avoided
gestures or tones of voice
considered uncontrolled
or effeminate. Facial
expressions and hand
movements were essential
for emphasis, and some
spoke more vigorously
than others, but few raised
their arms much beyond
shoulder height, or mimed.

RELATED HISTORIES
See also
EDUCATION & LITERACY
page 78

PROSE WRITING
page 86

3-SECOND BIOGRAPHIES
APULEIUS
125–180 CE
Popular orator and writer of
Latin prose

MARCUS TULLIUS CICERO
106–43 CE
Roman orator, politician,
theorist, and greatest
exponent of rhetoric in Latin

TACITUS
56–117 BCE
Senator and historian who
wrote a study on oratory

30-SECOND TEXT
Dunstan Lowe

Sculptures represent
speechmakers with
upraised palm or
pointing finger, and
always in the toga of
the dignified stateman.

70 BCE
Born, reputedly in Andes, a village near Mantua

C. 37 BCE
Completes *Eclogues*, a collection of ten pastoral poems

C. 36–29 BCE
Composes *Georgics*, a four-book didactic poem on Roman farming

C. 29–19 BCE
Works on the *Aeneid*, which is left unfinished at the poet's death

19 BCE
Dies at Brundisium (modern Brindisi), according to the ancient biographies, leaving instructions for the incomplete *Aeneid* to be burned; buried at Naples

4th century CE
Earliest surviving manuscript of Virgil's poetry

1427
Italian poet Maffeo Vegio adds a 13th book to the *Aeneid*, which is printed with Virgil's text in many early editions

1469
First printed edition of Virgil's works

1513
Gavin Douglas completes Scots translation of the *Aeneid* (published 1553)

1697
Publication of John Dryden's influential English translation of the *Aeneid*

VIRGIL

Publius Vergilius Maro (known in English as Virgil or Vergil) lived during the period of the civil wars at Rome, and witnessed the rise to power of Julius Caesar's great-nephew Octavian, who became the emperor Augustus. Although Virgil's earlier works were to prove influential (*Eclogues* played an important part in the development of the European tradition of pastoral poetry and *Georgics* show the continuing influence of Greek poetic models and, in their dedication to Octavian's cultural courtier Maecenas, Virgil's absorption into the circle of writers around the future emperor), his fame rests primarily on the epic *Aeneid*, which had a profound and lasting impact on Western art and literature.

Designed as a Roman counterpart to the Greek heroic epics of Homer, the *Iliad* and the *Odyssey* (the subjects of which are combined in the *Aeneid*'s opening words "arms and the man"), this 12-book narrative poem brings the most exalted literary genre of the ancient world into the realm of Roman history and politics. Prophetic passages throughout the poem look ahead from the mythological narrative of the Trojan Aeneas, legendary founder of the Roman race, to more contemporary events, anticipating the victories of Aeneas' supposed descendant Augustus. Virgil's celebration of the glorious destiny of Rome is not merely a triumphalist salute to imperial conquest, however; the poem also displays the human and personal cost of empire, including Aeneas' desertion of his lover, Dido (queen of Rome's historic enemy Carthage), in pursuit of his divinely ordained mission. Although the ghost of Aeneas' father Anchises memorably defines the Roman vocation as being "to spare the conquered, and to crush the proud in war," the *Aeneid* ends abruptly with Aeneas' impassioned slaughter of his defeated enemy, Turnus.

Highlights include Aeneas' account of the fall of Troy in Book 2, which contains the original warning against "Greeks bearing gifts" (applied here to the Trojan horse, in which Greek warriors lie concealed); the tragedy of Dido and Aeneas in Book 4, famously adopted as the subject for operas by Purcell and Berlioz; and Aeneas's visit to the underworld in Book 6, which was to provide inspiration for Dante's *Inferno* (where Virgil himself appears as the later poet's guide) and the early scenes of Milton's *Paradise Lost*. Recognized immediately as the supreme national epic of Rome, the *Aeneid* spawned an extensive tradition of Roman epic poetry, most notably Ovid's *Metamorphoses*, Lucan's *Civil War*, and Statius's *Thebaid*, all of which (especially the mythological stories of the *Metamorphoses*) enjoyed enormous popularity among later readers, writers, and artists.

Matthew Nicholls

PROSE WRITING

the 30-second history

Because the Latin language is precise and concrete, Roman prose writing became an effective and often stylish medium for communicating information and arguments. Whereas Roman poetry leaned heavily on Greek models and evolved partly through translations, prose writing had homegrown origins. As literacy spread, persuasive speechmaking—essential in the senate or courtroom, and central to elite education—lent its rhythmic patterns and rhetorical flourishes to other forms of writing. History evolved from brief civic "annals" (yearly records), but also commemorations of personal achievement: generals' bulletins, memoirs, and praise-speeches at funerals. Histories became nuanced narratives, producing emotional responses and enlivened with speeches. Biographies were a close relation, famously Suetonius's twelve lives of emperors. Novels in antiquity were a small, humble genre; in Latin, only Petronius's *Satyrica* and Apuleius's *Metamorphoses* survive, more scurrilous than the melodramatic Greek romances. Technical treatises, in which verbal artistry was less evident, imposed system on industries and sciences: Vitruvius's *On Architecture* and especially Pliny the Elder's encyclopedic *Natural History* remained valuable reference works into the Middle Ages and Renaissance.

RELATED HISTORY
See also
RHETORIC
page 82

3-SECOND SURVEY
Roman prose writing arose from two impulses: commemoration and persuasive speech. Rhetorical style influenced the artistry of all narrative forms including history, letters, and novels.

3-MINUTE EXCAVATION
The Romans used prose for texts requiring rapid dictation: in length both Livy's history and Cicero's collected letters far exceed most epics. Composing history was relatively respectable as politics, wars, and great individuals were deemed morally educational subjects. Philosophical works and studies of practical utility were also valuable. While no literary critic admits appreciation of humorous and obscene prose such as the novels or Seneca's satire on Claudius, there was evidently a readership.

3-SECOND BIOGRAPHIES
MARCUS TUILLIUS CICERO
106–43 BCE
Orator, statesman, and philosopher

PLINY THE ELDER
23–79 CE
Scholar and prolific author

30-SECOND TEXT
Dunstan Lowe

Cicero was—and is—widely considered the best Latin prose stylist: his speeches, philosophical works, and even private letters were published and savored.

CICERO

LATIN LYRIC POETRY

the 30-second history

Roads, bridges, aqueducts, and
sewers provide ample evidence of the Romans'
practical side, but they were also capable of
intense sensuality and even—although this
is denied in some older scholarship—of
passionate romanticism. This is apparent not
only in the fabulous mythological scenes of
Roman domestic wall-painting, but also in the
influential body of Latin lyric poetry, represented
chiefly by Catullus and Horace. The love
poems of Catullus, addressed to his capricious,
irresistible and unfaithful mistress Lesbia (the
name evokes the Greek lyric poetess Sappho of
Lesbos), range in tone from delicacy to pathos
to abusive obscenity; among the most famous
are the poet's lament for his girlfriend's dead
sparrow, and the so-called "kiss" poems, in
which Catullus reminds Lesbia of the shortness
of life as a spur to enjoy love while they still
can. This hedonistic philosophy was later
encapsulated by the greatest Roman lyric poet,
Horace, in the words *carpe diem* ("seize the
day"), which have served ever since as a motto
for those seeking to make the most of the
present. In addition to their erotic content,
Horace's *Odes* include political poems, drinking
songs, and meditations on the passing of time
and the immortality of poetry.

30-SECOND TEXT
Luke Houghton

*Lyric poetry was
originally intended
to have musical
accompaniment;
the longer poems may
have been crafted for
choral performance.*

INSCRIPTIONS & GRAFFITI

the 30-second history

Were the Romans able to read?

Scholars tend to pessimism in their view on literacy levels in the Roman Empire. Whatever the case may be, many Romans were able to write, producing lasting literature and everyday private documents such as letters and contracts. The Roman world was also profoundly inscribed, from its earliest times to the end of antiquity. Inscriptions adorned built structures and monuments such as the Pantheon, the famous triumphal arches of Rome, statue bases, altars, and milestones. Laws and decrees of the Senate were engraved in bronze and put on public display, and metal was the material of choice for military diplomas—the Romans' passports. Inscriptions on tombstones and funerary monuments helped Romans to remember and celebrate their ancestors' lives and achievements. The writing was on the wall, literally, in the case of graffiti or painted advertisements for political campaigns or games. It was on the floor, too (in mosaics), and on rooftops. There was also a darker side. Inscribed curses, sometimes wrapped around a chicken bone, were buried in the ground, so that spells could unfold their magic. Monumental or private, of lasting value or for quick consumption, writing in the public sphere was everywhere in the Roman world.

3-SECOND SURVEY
Inscriptions are expensive, so it is essential to keep the message short and pithy. Thus the Greek term for "inscription" epitomizes this concept: the epigram.

3-MINUTE EXCAVATION
Roman handwriting ("cursive script"), as found in the graffiti, wax tablets, and such, is notoriously hard to read for the uninitiated. Roman monumental lettering, however, has enjoyed lasting success due to the ease with which it is read. This particularly true for the famous *capitalis quadrata* ("squared upper-case"), developed during the reign of Augustus, and the *actuaria* ("swift'), a monumental font that resembles the strokes of a paint brush.

RELATED HISTORIES
See also
LATIN
page 76

TRIUMPHAL ARCHES
page 126

30-SECOND TEXT
Peter Kruschwitz

Roman square or inscriptional capitals were the lettering of choice for inscribing key Roman monuments, including the Arch of Titus, Trajan's Column, and the Pantheon.

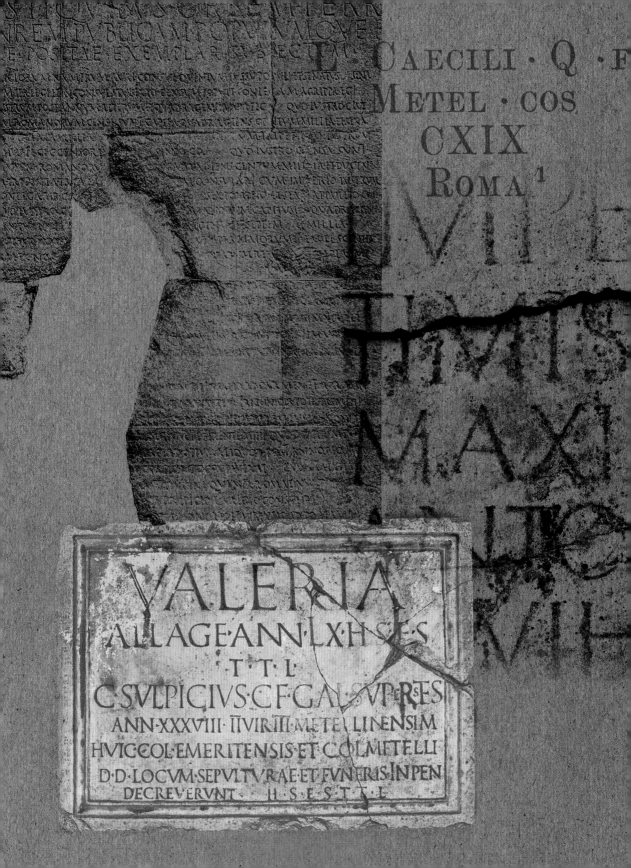

THOUGHT & BELIEF

THOUGHT & BELIEF
GLOSSARY

atheism Belief in no gods.

cult Literally the "care" offered to a deity through ritual, sacrifice, and worship.

deities The numberless gods that thronged the Roman world, from the great Olympian pantheon to the humble spirits of household shrines and crossroads.

divi filius Title meaning "son of the deified one" taken by the emperor Augustus in reference to his deified adoptive father Julius Caesar and used by several later emperors.

Epicureanism A branch of Greek philosophy following the teaching of Epicurus (fourth–third centuries BCE), who taught that the proper goal of philosophy was to secure a happy life.

lectisternium A banquet held to propitiate the gods, whose images were placed about on dining couches.

henotheism Belief in and worship of a single god, while accepting that a number of other deities may exist.

hippodrome The Greek term for a circus, an arena for chariot racing.

monotheism Belief in and worship of a single god to the exclusion of any other.

mystery cult A particular sort of Roman religion that involved initiating worshipers into secret "mysteries," which promised to reveal secrets of the cosmos—sometimes through terrifying ceremonies evoking death and rebirth. As these cults thrived in an atmosphere of mysterious secrecy, details of what exactly happened in their ceremonies are scarce.

numen The "expressed will" of a divinity or emperor—not itself a god, but a divine power of action. Worshiping the *numen* or *genius* (divine nature) of a living emperor was a delicate way for Romans to step round the awkward implications of ruler cult—though as time went on those scruples diminished, and were never strongly felt in parts of the empire.

On Divination A two-book philosophical work of 44 BCE by Cicero, discussing the interpretation of dreams, oracles, omens, and other signs.

polytheism Belief in and worship of a multiplicity of gods.

principate Name for the system of one-man rule established by Augustus, Rome's first emperor or *princeps* (a Latin word that translates roughly as "first citizen").

Republic Work of fourth century BCE Greek philosophy by Plato, which discussed the idea of justice and different forms of government; includes the idea of an ideal state governed by philosopher-kings.

ruler cult The Romans took from the Greeks the idea of offering sacrifice and divine honors to humans, including living rulers. The practice took off under the emperors; while "good" emperors avoided divine honors in Rome itself, encouraging sacrifice only to their *numen* or *genius*, they were often worshiped openly in the provinces and indeed by everyone after their death and deification.

sacrifice The very widespread ancient practice of making an offering to a god, often in the hope of a favor in return. The most expensive sacrifices, such as bulls, were a dramatic statement of piety and wealth and could lead to a feast of the butchered meat. At the other end of the scale were humble offerings of cakes or flowers to lesser deities.

syncretism The blending together of different (for example, Roman and native) gods who were felt to share characteristics—as is the case of Sulis-Minerva at Bath, England. An important element of religious integration.

Stoicism A branch of Greek philosophy (originally taught by Zeno, ca. 334–262 BCE, a philosopher in Athens, in a "stoa" or colonnade). Zeno's austere ethical teachings stress the importance of virtue and self-discipline.

tetrarchy The modern name for the college of four emperors introduced by Diocletian in 293 CE (one senior "Augustus" and one junior "Caesar" in each half of the empire, which was divided into east and west).

temple A type of building sacred to a god or gods and used as a venue for cult and sacrifice.

THE ROMAN PANTHEON

the 30-second history

Pantheon is a Greek word

meaning "all the gods," often understood to refer to the Greek deities known as the Olympian 12. The Roman pantheon may be thought of as a Roman "version" of these 12; the Roman goddess Venus, for example, stands in for the Greek Aphrodite. Certainly these 12 are singled out as a group when Livy describes a *lectisternium*—a ritual feast set out before statues of the gods—performed for them in 217 BCE. The gods shared couches in male-female pairs: Jupiter and Juno, Neptune and Minerva, Mars and Venus, Apollo and Diana, Vulcan and Vesta, Mercury and Ceres. The term Roman pantheon also means "all the Roman gods," an unimaginably large number. Deified emperors swelled out the ranks, as did "foreign" gods adopted by the Romans. Roman polytheists also invoked a huge variety of gods specific to a particular situation: take Spes, a goddess embodying Hope, or Lucina, goddess of childbirth, or even Sterculius, god of manure. The Pantheon is also the name of a famous Roman temple, built during Augustus's rule and probably intended to honor "all the gods;" the vagueness of its name allowed for the idea that Augustus deserved a place among these gods, while proclaiming nothing definite.

RELATED HISTORIES
See also
IMPORTED GODS
page 98

IMPERIAL CULT
page 104

3-SECOND BIOGRAPHIES
LIVY
59 BCE–17 CE
Historian who wrote a history of Rome running from its foundation to the present day

AUGUSTUS
63 BCE–14 CE
Rome's first emperor who established the Roman principate in 31 BCE

30-SECOND TEXT
Ailsa Hunt

3-SECOND SURVEY
The Roman pantheon embraced not only famous deities like Jupiter and Venus, but far shadier characters too, like Sterculius, god of manure.

3-MINUTE EXCAVATION
Popular particularly among philosophers, another approach to the Roman pantheon was to insist on the existence of one supreme god (perhaps called Jupiter), but also to acknowledge the existence of other subordinate deities (perhaps called demons or emanations). This kind of belief is often labelled henotheism, a Greek word meaning belief in one god, as distinct from monotheism, a Greek word meaning belief in only one god.

The Romans took the Greek term to refer collectively to their principal deities, headed by Jupiter; the temple known by that name may have been dedicated to "all the gods."

IMPORTED GODS

the 30-second history

The Roman world is so full of gods "that you might as easily bump into a god as a man": so jokes Quartilla, a character in a Roman novel. And it is easy to see where Quartilla is coming from. For the Romans—unlike many conquering nations—did not try to stamp out foreign cults and gods but tended to embrace them as their own, even if they were noticeably "un-Roman." Mithras, an imported Eastern god, featured in marble reliefs boasting a pointy Phrygian (today "Turkish") hat. Cybele was another prominent imported goddess whose tambourine-heavy processions led by castrated priests were a shock to many Roman observers. Other gods entered Roman culture through the process of syncretism, the blending of a foreign and a Roman deity. Sulis Minerva, worshiped at Bath, England, combines the Celtic god Sul with the Roman Minerva. Hermanubis, another syncretic god, was surely more challenging to Roman imagination: he had the torso of the messenger god Hermes, but the head of the Egyptian jackal-headed god Anubis. Roman welcome of new gods had few limits: but those gods whose worshipers were themselves intolerant of other gods, like the Jews and Christians, could be met with hostility.

3-SECOND SURVEY
Roman polytheists openly adopted the new gods they discovered as their empire expanded—the more the better.

3-MINUTE EXCAVATION
Embracing foreign gods as their own might make Roman polytheists look surprisingly religiously tolerant, but being open to new gods was also understood to benefit the state. It was sometimes argued that the reason the Romans ruled the ancient world was because they alone worshiped all gods. Cybele herself was imported from modern-day Turkey in 204 BCE after consultation of a religious text suggested that this might help Rome against its political rival Carthage.

RELATED HISTORIES
See also
EMPIRE & EXPANSION
page 26

THE ROMAN PANTHEON
page 96

CHRISTIANITY
page 100

3-SECOND BIOGRAPHIES
OVID
43 BCE—ca. 18 CE
Roman poet whose works were highly influential as a source of classical mythology

APOLLONIUS OF TYANA
fl. first century CE
Orator and philosopher from Roman province of Cappadoccia, Asia Minor

TITUS FLAVIUS JOSEPHUS
37—100 CE
Romano-Jewish scholar, historian, and hagiographer

30-SECOND TEXT
Ailsa Hunt

The Roman ability to accept different gods as forms of the same thing helped bring cohesion to a huge and diverse empire.

CHRISTIANITY

the 30-second history

3-SECOND SURVEY
At first a ridiculed minority, Christians could scarcely have imagined in their early days that, three centuries on, a Christian would rule the Roman world.

3-MINUTE EXCAVATION
Naturally enough, Roman pagans at first thought of Christianity as a Jewish sect. Romans had long been hostile to Judaism—partly owing to Jewish insistence on worshiping one god—and transferred their prejudices about Judaism to Christianity. For example, Roman pagans used to accuse Jews of worshiping a donkey in the temple in Jerusalem, an accusation repeated in a striking Roman graffito that shows a Christian worshiping a crucified donkey.

What was it that led Christians in the Roman empire to the gory fate of being thrown into the arena to be fed to hungry lions? As a minority religious group, which at first worshiped in private houses, not churches, Christians were vulnerable to the spread of terrible rumors: the communion meal, the ritual eating of Christ's "body" and "blood" was, for example, interpreted as cannibalism. More surprisingly, perhaps, Christians were often seen as atheists: by insisting on worshiping one god alone, Christians were dangerous disparagers of the gods who could bring divine anger on the state. Yet the religion was obviously deeply attractive to many: by 312 CE a Christian emperor, Constantine, ruled the Roman world and Christianity had spread like wildfire. The Christian promise of a resurrected afterlife was surely important: images on the walls of Christian tombs in Rome are thought to represent this promise, such as Jonah being rescued from the belly of a whale. Christianity perhaps also appealed ideologically to "downtrodden" groups in Rome, like slaves and women: a famous passage from a letter by Paul controversially denies any difference between slaves and free, or between men and women.

RELATED HISTORIES
See also
CONSTANTINE
page 102

DEATH & THE AFTERLIFE
page 110

TOMBS
page 132

3-SECOND BIOGRAPHY
PAUL (ORIGINALLY SAUL)
fl. 1st century CE
Jew who converted to Christianity and became a missionary who preached throughout the Mediterranean world

30-SECOND TEXT
Ailsa Hunt

Christians commonly attracted hostility in the Roman world and feeding them to the lions was (at times) considered to be a form of entertainment.

Born, the son of Flavius Valerius Constantius and Helena

On his father's death, acclaimed emperor by the army at York

Victorious at the Battle of the Milvian Bridge in northern Rome, defeating his rival Maxentius who drowned in the river Tiber

Published, along with his then ally and colleague Licinius, the Edict of Milan proclaiming religious tolerance across the empire

Victorious at the Battle of Chrysopolis in Bithynia (modern-day Turkey), defeating Licinius, who had become his final imperial rival

Called the First Council of Nicaea

Officially founded Constantinople as the new capital of the Roman empire

Died from illness and was buried in the Church of the Holy Apostles in Constantinople

CONSTANTINE

Just outside York Minster stands an imposing bronze statue of a man seated on a throne. It is not, as you might expect, an illustrious archbishop. This is Constantine the Great. He has earned this prominent spot because it was in the Roman town of Eboracum (today York, England) that Constantine was acclaimed as emperor in 306 CE. It is a fitting spot, too, because Constantine is famous above all for becoming the first Christian emperor of Rome. His conversion moment is said to have been a vision he witnessed the night before a decisive battle in 312 CE. Looking up to the sun, Constantine saw a cross shining above it, and written in Greek the words "by this sign conquer."

From this beginning Constantine went on to shape the early Christian church. The Edict of Milan, a political agreement he secured only a year later, ensured religious tolerance across the empire, a blessing for the long-persecuted Christians. Constantine also ordered the building of Jerusalem's famous Church of the Holy Sepulchre and called the First Council of Nicaea, which established a statement of Christian belief still used today (the Nicene Creed). Indeed, Constantine is even revered as a saint in Orthodox Christianity. Yet the "purity" of Constantine's Christian faith is very much debated. Throughout his reign imagery of the sun god Apollo—a favoured god in Constantine's pre-Christian days—continued to appear, but now combined with Christian iconography. Was Constantine worshiping Christ alone, or a combination of the two?

Constantine came to power within a tetrarchy. Yet through a series of protracted civil wars eliminating his co-rulers, by 324 CE Constantine was sole ruler of the Roman world. The strength of his personal ambition and vision for the empire are particularly visible in his building projects: famously he founded a new city, on the site of Byzantium in modern-day Turkey, which he boldly named "New Rome." The name, however, never caught on, and soon the city was called Constantinople (later Istanbul): a hippodrome that seated more than 80,000 spectators and a lavish imperial palace proclaimed Constantine's power. Moreover, despite his provocative "New Rome," the old Rome was hardly ignored. Visitors today marvel at the Arch of Constantine, while the famous St. Peter's Basilica occupies the site of a church Constantine founded.

Ailsa Hunt

IMPERIAL CULT

the 30-second history

When a comet streaked across the sky at the funeral games for Julius Caesar in 44 BCE many took this as definitive proof that the dead dictator had become a god. Nor was it long before Augustus, Caesar's adopted son and first emperor of Rome, began to style himself "son of a god" (*divi filius*) on his coinage. Augustus' subjects were keen to express their political allegiance to the new emperor and his unique political position, and one way to do this was to use religious language and actions to present him as divine in some way; here the ruler cult offered to Greek kings in the previous two centuries provided a useful model. Yet there was still much hesitancy about the nature of Augustus's divine status. The inhabitants of Narbo in modern day France set up an altar to the "divine spirit" (*numen*) of Augustus, rather than directly to the emperor himself. After Augustus, however, such caution was mostly thrown to the wind, as more and more members of the imperial family received sacrifice or worship on more and more occasions. When, for example, Nero's wife Poppaea gave birth, priests sacrificed in thanksgiving for the safe delivery; when the baby died aged four months, the infant was deified and received her own priest and temple.

RELATED HISTORIES
See also
JULIUS CAESAR
page 22

IMPERIAL GOVERNMENT
page 24

COINAGE & CURRENCY
page 60

3-SECOND BIOGRAPHIES
JULIUS CAESAR
100–44 BCE
Politician and dictator of Rome

AUGUSTUS
63 BCE–14 CE
Established the Roman principate and became Rome's first emperor

NERO
37–68 CE
Fifth emperor of Rome, remembered mostly for his insanity and brutality

30-SECOND TEXT
Ailsa Hunt

Imperial cult gained emperors political and religious loyalty and was a vital unifying factor in the large, diverse empire.

3-SECOND SURVEY
The Roman emperor enjoyed a position of unique power; the imperial cult helped to express what made him so different and somehow "more than mortal."

3-MINUTE EXCAVATION
We might think that the ability to see and touch an emperor would convince most he was hardly a god. Yet Romans placed positive emphasis on the emperor being a "present god." Arguably it made more sense to entreat an "immediate" god like Augustus, rather than a distant one like Apollo. Yet things probably felt different for the emperors themselves: Vespasian supposedly joked on his deathbed "Oh no, I think I'm becoming a god!"

ASTROLOGY & DIVINATION

the 30-second history

3-SECOND SURVEY
Messages from the gods were everywhere in the Roman world, be it in the distant stars, or the entrails of a sacrificed sheep.

3-MINUTE EXCAVATION
Not everyone was convinced by the arts of astrology and divination. Roman admiral Claudius Pulcher threw his sacred chickens overboard when they failed to accept offered sacrificial grain, saying "If they won't eat, let them drink"—then lost the battle. In his dialog *On Divination* Cicero mocks those who want to read divine messages into the behavior of all animals. "Should I," he jokes, "think that the state is in great danger if mice gnaw my copy of Plato's *Republic*? After all, gnawing is the main business of mice."

For many people today, astrology takes up no more space in their lives than the horoscope in the average newspaper. But in the Roman world, astrology was popular in all strata of society. Emperor Tiberius was famous—indeed infamous—for his reliance on his court astrologer Thrasyllus. At the other end of the scale, astrological signs were also important for ordinary Romans involved in the hugely popular mystery cult of the god Mithras; the ram Aries, for example, is mentioned in graffiti from a shrine to Mithras in Rome. Similarly, divination was an everyday practice central to Roman politics. It involved reading divine messages in, for example, the behavior of birds or the appearance of the entrails of sacrificed animals. State priests were employed to "test out" the will of the gods by such means before politicians undertook proposed courses of action. A famous mythological example has Romulus and Remus as the first Romans to make a political decision in this way. Fighting over the hill on which they would found Rome, Romulus and Remus decided to observe the birds from their chosen hills. Romulus saw 12 vultures, Remus only 6: this meant Romulus' decision was final.

RELATED HISTORIES
See also
FOUNDATION
page 16

SITE OF ROME
page 18

INSCRIPTIONS & GRAFFITI
page 90

3-SECOND BIOGRAPHIES
CICERO
106–43 BCE
Roman orator, politician, and author of philosophical works

TIBERIUS
42 BCE–37 CE
Rome's second emperor (ruled 14–37 CE)

30-SECOND TEXT
Ailsa Hunt

Reading the signs was a Roman preoccupation, and interpretation of divine messages was the official task of augurs to tell whether a political or military course of action was approved by the gods.

PHILOSOPHY

the 30-second history

Stoicism and Epicureanism were giants among the many philosophical theories popular in the Roman world. In a society that relied heavily on the distinction between slave and free, Stoics controversially claimed that we are all slaves to our emotions. Developing self-control to overcome destructive emotions and achieve peace of mind, particularly when facing death, was central to Stoic ethics. Moralizing anecdotes about "noble" suicides were popular, like that of the gladiator who, having no other option, calmly choked himself to death on a toilet sponge. Yet Stoicism wasn't only about a way of life. Stoics also taught about the nature of the world which, they argued, was pervaded by the divine as man is by his soul. Epicureans differed in this regard: for them, the world was composed of atoms and void. Their ethical teaching was that pleasure is the highest good, but this did not mean, as their rivals claimed, continual indulgence in bodily pleasures. Lucretius, for example, taught that sex was best if engaged in unemotionally. This was because Epicureans believed the way to achieve pleasure was to become free from emotion and fear, especially fear of death and—more controversially—fear of the gods.

RELATED HISTORIES
See also
SLAVERY
page 38

DEATH & THE AFTERLIFE
page 110

3-SECOND SURVEY
For the Romans, philosophy taught you about the nature of the universe, how to spend your time in it, and how to take your leave.

3-MINUTE EXCAVATION
Roman philosophy was heavily indebted to Greek philosophy. The Epicureans, for example, were named after their Greek founder Epicurus whom Lucretius paints as a semi-divine figure in his great poem "On the Nature of the Universe." In this poem Lucretius also bemoans the fact that the "poverty" of the Latin language does not allow him to express Greek philosophical concepts easily and fully.

3-SECOND BIOGRAPHIES
LUCRETIUS
fl. first century BCE
Epicurean philosopher who wrote the epic poem "On the Nature of the Universe"

EPICURUS
341–270 BCE
Greek philosopher and founder of the school of Epicureanism. Enquired into how to lead a good life, existing free from pain and enjoying the fruits of human society.

30-SECOND TEXT
Ailsa Hunt

Greek philosophical doctrines adopted and adapted by Roman authors became the basis of much Western philosophy.

DEATH &
THE AFTERLIFE

the 30-second history

On several Roman tombstones
are inscribed the letters "NF F NS NC." They
represent an abbreviation of a Latin tag
meaning "I didn't exist, I existed, I don't exist,
I don't care." These joky tombstones must have
been favorites of philosophers like Lucretius
who also insisted that death is nothing to us.
Indeed, Lucretius himself is famous for the
"symmetry argument," similar to that of the
tombstones, namely if not being alive before we
were born didn't bother us, why should we
worry about our non-existence post mortem?
Most people, however, were clearly more
concerned about the afterlife: thousands of
Roman tombstone inscriptions are addressed to
the "gods of the underworld." In the *Aeneid*
Virgil paints a famous picture of this underworld
with sinners being tortured—Sisyphus, for
example, pushing his rock up the hill—while
blessed souls enjoy themselves in Elysium. The
afterlife also seems to have been a particular
concern of mystery cults into which ancient
Romans were initiated, but because these cults
were meant to be mysterious, the evidence is
sparse. Some of this evidence leaves tantalizing
traces of people's beliefs, such as one
inscription that reveals an initiate of the Isis cult
asking underworld gods to refresh his dead wife
with "cold water."

3-SECOND SURVEY
Depending on personal
beliefs, death in ancient
Rome either was, or
wasn't, the be-all and
end-all.

3-MINUTE EXCAVATION
If the nature of the
afterlife was uncertain,
many Roman poets hoped
to secure for themselves
literary immortality.
Horace boasted that in
writing his poems he had
raised a monument more
lasting than bronze and so
he would never completely
die. Ovid also ends his
Metamorphoses with a
boast that his poems will
always be read, leading up
to the final triumphant
word of his great poem,
which translates as
"I will live!"

RELATED HISTORIES
See also
LATIN LYRIC POETRY
page 88

INSCRIPTIONS & GRAFFITI
page 90

TOMBS
page 132

3-SECOND BIOGRAPHIES
LUCRETIUS
fl. first century BCE
Philosopher who wrote the
epic poem "On the Nature of
the Universe"

VIRGIL
70–19 BCE
Poet who wrote three major
works: the *Eclogues*, the
Georgics, and the *Aeneid*

30-SECOND TEXT
Ailsa Hunt

*For Romans of all
social strata, relief
carvings and Roman
square capitals
provided the means to
commemorate
deceased family
members and friends.*

ARCHITECTURE, MONUMENTS & ART

ARCHITECTURE, MONUMENTS & ART
GLOSSARY

basilica Aisled halls, often found in the forum of a Roman town, using for banking, law courts, and other civic business.

"bread and circuses" *panem et circenses*— a shorthand for the emperors' generosity toward the urban population of Rome through the provision of cheap food and free entertainment.

capital The topmost element of a column, between the shaft and the lower element (architrave) of the entablature. The easiest way to tell Doric, Ionic, and Corinthian orders apart is to look at their capitals.

catacombs Extensive galleries of underground tombs cut into the rocks around Rome from the second century CE, often by Christian and Jewish communities.

cella The inner chamber of a Roman temple, in which the statue of the god or goddess might be housed.

columbaria Literally "dovecots," burial chambers whose walls were lined with niches for the burial urns of the cremated poor and middling inhabitants of Rome.

column A vertical load-bearing pillar: the basic unit of classical architecture, developed into different orders.

Composite order A Roman variation of the Corinthian order, combining its foliage with the scrolling volutes of the Ionic.

concrete One of the great Roman contributions to architecture: a versatile, robust material that can be molded into any shape and even made to set underwater.

Corinthian order A columnar order whose elaborate capitals, with (massed) tiers of carved acanthus foliage, are easy to spot. Favored by Roman architects for its elaboration and richness.

Doric order A columnar order consisting of massive fluted columns terminating in a plain capital, with the frieze of the entablature divided between metope panels and a grooved decoration called triglyphs.

entablature The horizontal superstructure running above the column capitals in a Classical building. Each order specified a form of decoration for the surfaces of this element.

fresco Wall decoration painted directly onto wet plaster. Roman houses often featured frescos of mythological scenes, or architectural perspectives.

Ionic order An architectural order whose columns are more slender in proportion to their height than the Doric, with curving scrolled volutes at the corners of their capitals.

On Architecture Ten-book Latin treatise on architecture by Augustan architect Vitruvius. Covers theory, materials, means of construction, the disposition of public and private buildings, and military technology.

manes The Roman spirits of the dead; *manes* could mean something like the "soul" or "shade" of the departed.

mausoleum An elaborate monumental tomb for an individual or dynasty. Named after the tomb of King Mausolus at Halicarnassus (modern Bodrum in Turkey), one of the seven wonders of the ancient world.

orders Architectural styles consisting of columns plus their capitals and entablatures. The choice of order—usually Doric, Ionic, or Corinthian—entailed a set of rules of form and proportion and set the "rhythm" or overall style of a building.

piers Masonry supports carrying the weight of a vaulted roof (more massive than columns).

podium The platform on which a temple or other structure might stand, raising it up from ground level.

tesserae The tiny cubes of stone or glass that were laid in patterns to make up a mosaic.

Triumphatores A *triumphator* was a victorious Roman general who had earned the right to an elaborate victory parade through Rome called a "triumph"—the ultimate celebration of military and political success.

templum Technically not a "temple" building but a space inaugurated by a sacred ritual, in which a shrine might be located.

Tuscan order A plain, simple columnar order, not unlike the Doric.

veristic A style of Roman portrait sculpture that emphasized "warts and all" realism, favoring signs of aging to imply authority.

COLUMNAR ORDERS

the 30-second history

Greek temples, such as the Parthenon in Athens, base their whole visual language on the proportions and ornament of the different columnar "orders" (the column and its associated superstructure or "entablature"). Roman architects appreciated this heritage and the rules that governed the use of each order: the sturdy, masculine Doric; the slender, feminine Ionic (Vitruvius writes that its scrolled capitals were like a lady's "graceful curling hair"); the more elaborate Corinthian, with its carved acanthus-leaf foliage. The Corinthian order and its near-relative, the Composite, particularly appealed to the Roman love of detail. It additionally had the advantage of being totally symmetrical and as a result useful for all sorts of structures. Roman architects therefore made heavy use of these orders, but gradually took the column a long way from its roots. Whereas in Greek architecture the column was a structural element, transmitting the weight of a building's roof into its foundations, in Roman architecture, massive concrete piers and vaults often carried the weight, meaning columns or columnar elements could be deployed as decorative details—in ever more elaborate arrays—without actually holding anything up.

3-SECOND SURVEY
Roman architects borrowed the columnar orders of the Greeks, but adapted them to their own aesthetic ends, devising new forms like the Tuscan and Composite orders.

3-MINUTE EXCAVATION
Roman architects used decorative tiers of columns on all manner of structures—fountain houses, gateways, and especially theater stage backdrops. The Colosseum is a fine example: here the "engaged" half columns are mere surface decoration, without structural purpose, and a different order (Tuscan, Ionic, or Corinthian) is used on each of the three arcaded stories. In many buildings the use of light and shade, colorful marbles, and novel effects like spiral fluting added further visual effect.

RELATED HISTORIES
See also
THE COLOSSEUM & CIRCUS MAXIMUS
page 118

TEMPLES
page 120

TRIUMPHAL ARCHES
page 126

3-SECOND BIOGRAPHIES
APOLLODORUS OF DAMASCUS
fl. second century CE
Greek engineer and Trajan's chief architect

30-SECOND TEXT
Matthew Nicholls

Use of the column as a decorative, almost baroque feature, although disliked by Vitruvius and other purists, meant that Roman architecture had a distinctive visual identity.

THE COLOSSEUM & CIRCUS MAXIMUS

the 30-second history

Purpose-built structures for entertainment show how seriously Roman leaders took the "bread and circuses" task of keeping their city populations happy. Rome's buildings for gladiatorial combat (the Colosseum) and chariot-racing (the Circus Maximus) were, appropriately, the largest and finest in the world. The Colosseum was not Rome's first amphitheater, but once it was built in the 70s CE it became an instant classic; it is still an emblem of the city. Its oval arena overlays complex basements holding combatants, animals, and props for the arena; above ground its tiers of seats reflected Rome's social structure—the more important you were, the closer to the action you sat. Built by the military-minded emperor, Vespasian, in what had been the private grounds of Nero's hated palace, this 50,000+ seater stadium was a careful, populist gesture, signaling the new dynasty's common touch and vigorous Roman tastes. The nearby Circus Maximus fills a long, narrow valley between the Palatine and Aventine hills. Horse- and chariot-racing were held here from the earliest times; by the second century CE the Circus had been successively rebuilt to hold up to a quarter of a million spectators, reflecting the huge popularity of the races (and gambling) that took place there.

3-SECOND SURVEY
Elaborate, purpose-built stadiums for gladiatorial combat and chariot-racing show how emperors cultivated the popularity of the games in Rome.

3-MINUTE EXCAVATION
The name "Colosseum" comes from a huge statue (or "Colossus") of the emperor Nero, remodeled into the sun god after his downfall, which eventually lent its name to the huge stadium—officially the Flavian Amphitheater—nearby. Imperial poets dutifully praised the generosity of games-giving emperors, but the racier love-poet Ovid said that the Circus, with its tight-packed seating, was a good place to pick up girls. Both buildings were imitated across the empire by towns eager to boost their reputations.

RELATED HISTORIES
See also
ENTERTAINMENT & SPORT
page 68

3-SECOND BIOGRAPHIES
CALIGULA
12–41 CE
Emperor (ruled 37–41 CE) notoriously devoted to chariot racing, apparently to the point of trying at one time to make his horse a consul

30-SECOND TEXT
Matthew Nicholls

Rome's two largest venues for staging public spectacles and entertainment were central to the leisure of the populace, and became the model for similar structures throughout the empire.

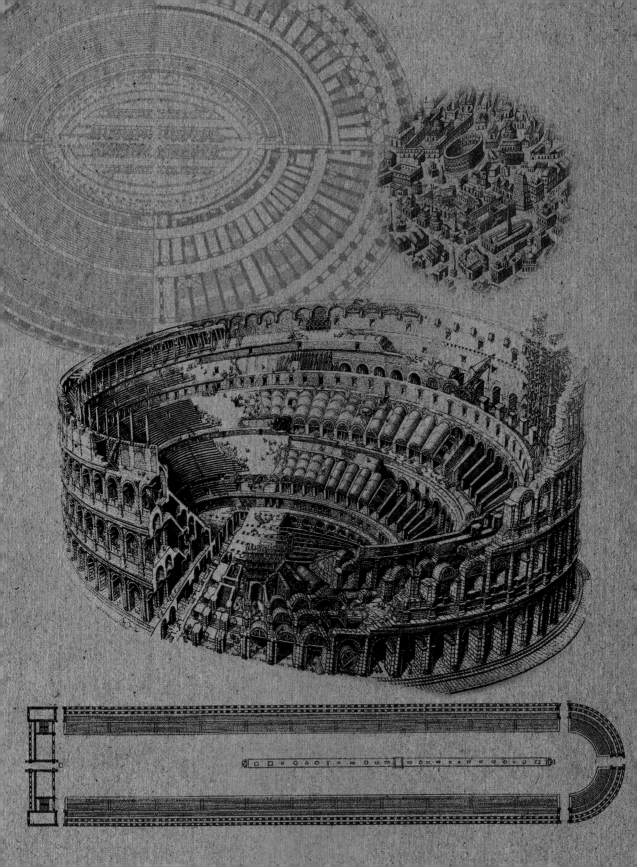

TEMPLES

the 30-second history

Religion permeated the public and private spaces of the Roman world. Homes, workplaces, and crossroads contained shrines and altars, while adherents of some cults (like that of Mithras) met in enclosed, secretive chambers. The principal gods, however, required more substantial, public premises. The Latin word *templum* actually means a consecrated space: anywhere the senate met, for example, had to be a *templum*. In general, though, the English word "temple" refers to public buildings erected for the honor and worship of the gods. These, with many variations over time and space, conform to a recognizable architectural pattern. The Romans adopted the Greek template of a rectangular building with a porch, an inner chamber or *cella*, and a roof supported by rows of stone columns. From their Etruscan neighbors they took the idea of placing the temple on a high podium, approached by a tall flight of steps, often with a sacrificial altar at the front, and much of the priestly ritual that made use of this dramatic architecture. Such sacred buildings gave Roman towns their architectural character: within Rome itself the Forum contained several temples, while from the adjacent Capitoline Hill the great temple of Jupiter Optimus Maximus overlooked the city.

3-SECOND SURVEY
Temples provided magnificent, conspicuous public buildings for the worship of Rome's protecting gods.

3-MINUTE EXCAVATION
Roman architects could experiment with traditional temple forms. The Pantheon in Rome, sacred to all the gods, is a fine example: from the front, this resembles a conventional temple with a columnar porch. But in place of the rectangular *cella* is an enormous round space, still one of the largest concrete domes in the world: one ancient writer said that it resembled the vault of the heavens. Like several temples, it has been preserved by conversion into a church.

RELATED HISTORIES
See also
COLUMNAR ORDERS
page 116

THE FORUM
page 122

CONCRETE & VAULT
page 152

3-SECOND BIOGRAPHIES
HADRIAN
117–138 CE
Emperor who oversaw the building of the Pantheon

NUMA POMPILIUS
d. 673 BCE
Legendary second king of Rome (ruled 715–673 BCE) to whom Romans attributed much of the city's ancient religious lore

30-SECOND TEXT
Matthew Nicholls

The temple was the focal point of religious worship until the late fourth century CE and is one of the most iconic examples of classical architecture.

THE FORUM

the 30-second history

In its earliest phase, Rome was a cluster of hilltop villages. Their inhabitants needed a central place to meet and transact business, and to bury their dead, and chose the marshy area enclosed between four of the hills. As Rome expanded, this area was drained and paved in the seventh century BCE and started to acquire its first monuments, temples, and public buildings. Thus it became the Forum, the city's center of commercial, civic, political, and religious life. As Rome's size, wealth, and sense of itself as a capital city grew, shops and houses were gradually cleared to make way for grander public buildings. Contact with the magnificent royal cities of the Greek east resulted in the construction from the second century BCE of Greek-style "basilicas," colonnaded halls flanking the long sides of the Forum for banking, law courts, and public business. The transition from republic to empire saw another transformation. Julius Caesar began changes completed by his heir, the first emperor Augustus: their grandiose rebuilding schemes posed as respectful restoration, but in reality transformed the Forum into a monumental precinct that honored the new dynasty and cemented its place at the heart of every type of activity conducted there.

RELATED HISTORIES
See also
FOUNDATION
page 16

TEMPLES
page 120

3-SECOND SURVEY
The forum was the center of a Roman city, housing many of its chief temples and civic buildings.

3-MINUTE EXCAVATION
Roman towns from Britain to Africa had a forum at their heart. The relatively well-preserved later layers of Rome's Forum make it hard to perceive its developmental history. Studying the fora of provincial towns, which were often modeled on that of Rome, helps us to interpret how Rome's Forum was understood and imitated. Over time ambitious provincial towns, including Pompeii followed Rome's lead, closing their fora to traffic, removing messy commercial activities, and filling the space with imperial monuments, statues, and arches.

3-SECOND BIOGRAPHY
AUGUSTUS
63 BCE–14 CE
Rome's first emperor, who refurbished the main Forum, completed Caesar's "imperial Foum," and added another

30-SECOND TEXT
Matthew Nicholls

Rome's Forum was the communal hub of the city, where business, commerce, religious activities, and the administration of justice was carried out.

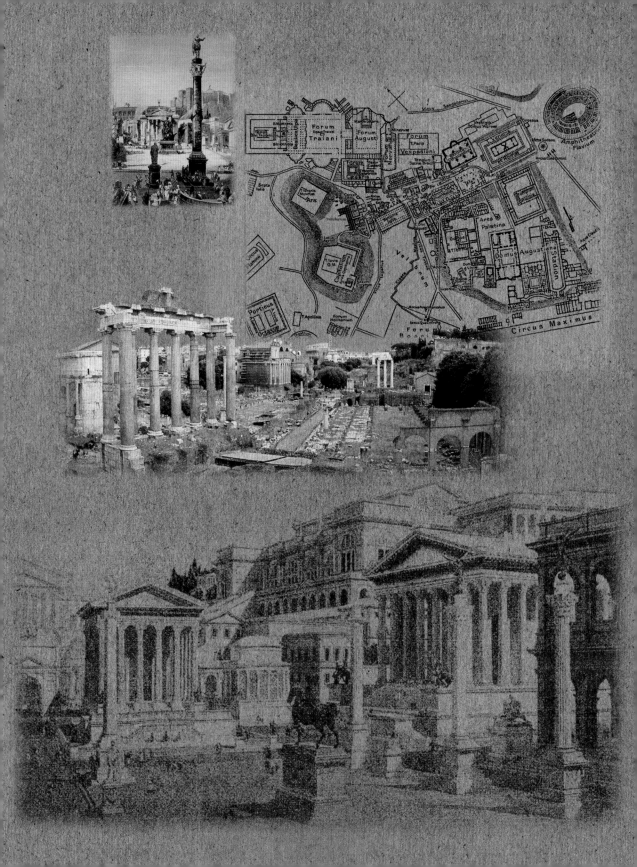

58 BCE
Born Livia Drusilla

43–2 BCE
Married to Tiberius Claudius Nero, her cousin

November 16th, 42 BCE
Birth of her first son, the future emperor Tiberius

39 BCE
Divorced her husband, though pregnant, in order to marry Octavian (the future Augustus), which would eventually secure her future as the first empress of Rome

38 BCE
Birth of her second son, Nero Claudius Drusus

31 BCE
Battle of Actium— Octavian becomes sole ruler of Roman world

23 BCE
Death of Augustus's heir Marcellus

2 CE
Death of Augustus's heir Lucius Caesar

4 CE
Death of Augustus's heir Gaius Caesar

9 CE
Potential heir Agrippa Posthumus exiled

14 CE
Death of Augustus and Agrippa Posthumus; accession of Tiberius as emperor. Will of Augustus grants Livia the honorific title of Augusta

16 CE
Becomes first woman to have her portrait appear on provincial coins

19–20 CE
Livia possibly involved in the murky events around the death of Germanicus and the trial and suicide of governor Piso: another attempt to remove a potential rival?

20 CE
Tiberius grants Livia a series of honors. Her continued attempts to influence his rule opened a serious rift between them

26 CE
Tiberius abandoned Rome, allegedly to avoid Livia's influence

29 CE
Dies. Tiberius forbids her deification

42 CE
Deified by her grandson the emperor Claudius. He bestows the name Diva Augusta on her

LIVIA DRUSILLA

Ancient Rome was a man's

world: all offices of state were for men and elected only by the male citizen body; women remained under the nominal control of their father or husband, and women's work was traditionally confined to the household.

When Rome's old republican constitution fell apart, replaced by a single emperor, there was therefore no established public role for the women of the imperial house. Subject to intense scrutiny, vested with a degree of informal power through access to and influence over the emperor, and above all necessary to produce the heirs vital to dynastic rule, the role of empress had to be developed more or less from scratch.

It was Augustus's wife Livia—as wife, mother, grandmother, great- and great-great-grandmother to Rome's first five emperors—who created the model for later imperial women. By establishing a role for imperial women she also created a public role for women within the state and society more broadly: the statues of hundreds of female patrons and benefactors in Roman towns across the empire all owe something to Livia, both in their appearance and in their very existence as public statements of female power.

Livia was not Augustus's first wife, and he wasn't her first husband. When Augustus married her she was already pregnant and had to arrange a hurried divorce. She and Augustus had no children together, leaving his daughter and her two sons to establish the family line—a situation that worked very imperfectly and went through endless changes, exiles, deaths, marriages, and divorces (darkly attributed to her malign agency by later writers) before her son Tiberius eventually became emperor, to no one's particular joy except hers, in 14 CE.

Although Livia could be ruthless in dispatching family members who fell short or got in the way of her aims (one grandson called her "Ulysses in petticoats"), her steadfast presence at Augustus's side, her intelligence, tact, and steely determination, made her a formidable partner in his labors, while her unimpeachable public conduct allowed him to present his family as a moral and social model for the Roman world.

As the Julio-Claudian dynasty of emperors continued to unfold over the decades she was seen as its revered ancestress, accorded unprecedented honors in her lifetime and eventually deified in 42 CE more than a decade after her death in 29 CE—after falling out with Tiberius—as "the divine Augusta."

Matthew Nicholls

TRIUMPHAL ARCHES

the 30-second history

The triumphal arch is a distinctively Roman structure, with no functional purpose except commemoration or the marking of a particular place. Their associations with military victory and imperial power, and their suitability as platforms for sculpture and relief carving, made arches popular among Rome's rulers and in later ages—Marble Arch in London and the Arc de Triomphe in Paris are based on the Roman arch. Triumphal arches stood over the Triumphal Way in Rome, a processional route through the city that was taken by generals whose victory fulfilled the strict criteria for the award of this most exalted of honors. *Triumphatores*—after Augustus, always emperors and their families—who wanted a permanent record of their moment of glory could erect an archway over the road, decorated with records of their victory and linking them with their illustrious predecessors. Gradually, such arches came to be part of the wider repertoire of commemorative architecture, and were used to mark the start and end of major roads and bridges, places of religious significance, and boundaries. Covered with relief carvings of battles, deifications, gods, and victory processions, and topped with statues, they confidently projected imperial power.

RELATED HISTORIES
See also
THE FORUM
page 122

STATUES
page 130

TOMBS
page 132

3-SECOND BIOGRAPHIES
TITUS
39–81 CE
Military commander (later emperor) commemorated by the Arch of Titus

SEPTIMIUS SEVERUS
145–211 CE
First African Roman Emperor, commemorated by Rome's second surviving triumphal arch

CONSTANTINE
272–337 CE
The first Christian emperor; his is the most recent of Rome's surviving triumphal arches

30-SECOND TEXT
Matthew Nicholls

What better way to mark military triumph than with a victory arch built to span a road?

3-SECOND SURVEY
Set in prominent and significant locations and built on an impressive scale, triumphal arches commemorated Roman victories with elaborate architectural swagger.

3-MINUTE EXCAVATION
The Arch of Constantine in Rome, adjacent to the Colosseum, is a particularly important one. It bent the rules from the outset, as it was erected in 315 CE to mark Constantine's victory in a civil war, rather than over a foreign enemy. Its decoration, largely of fine panels removed from earlier imperial monuments, is supplemented by far less skillful contemporary sculpture. Is this a hasty bodge-job, the beginning of the end of "realistic" classical art, or the dawn of a new medieval aesthetic?

MOSAIC

the 30-second history

The Romans took the idea of mosaics—like so many other forms of art—from the Greeks, who, since at least the fifth century BCE, had been laying mosaics of pebbles and then of specially cut cubes (tesserae) of colored marble or stone. Rome's highly developed towns and buildings, its appetite for fashionable decoration, and the pan-Mediterranean extent of its trading networks saw mosaic developed to new heights of sophistication and luxury. At its simplest, mosaic was a hardwearing, relatively cheap floor covering. Made from thousands of tesserae, it could cover a large room in a geometric pattern that would withstand heavy usage and was impermeable to water—ideal, then, for the thousands of bathhouses in Roman towns and cities. Various forms of mosaic were in fashion at different times and places; in imperial Rome and Italy black-and-white geometric patterns were common, whereas many provincial workshops, particularly those of north Africa, developed a taste for spectacular colored mosaics containing pictures of gods, people, gladiators, chariot races, abundant fruit and vegetables, and much else. Mosaic—especially using colored glass, with shells and other additions—could also be used to decorate walls, fountain grottoes, and even ceilings in Roman villas and gardens.

3-SECOND SURVEY
Mosaics, made of stone or glass laid in patterns and pictures, were a common floor covering in the Roman world and could also be used to embellish walls and ceilings.

3-MINUTE EXCAVATION
Although most mosaic was a mass-produced and not particularly prestigious floor covering, at the high end of the market it could be used to create real works of art. Famous examples include painterly images of doves drinking from a fountain or an illusionistic "unswept floor" for dining rooms, showing the remains of a rich banquet.

RELATED HISTORY
See also
BATHS & HYPOCAUST
page 146

3-SECOND BIOGRAPHY
SOSUS OF PERGAMUM
fl. second century BCE
Greek mosaicist named by Pliny the Elder, famous for his realistic, painterly works

30-SECOND TEXT
Matthew Nicholls

Painstakingly created mosaics use tesserae to build up realistic effects of color and shadow—some floor mosaics have been found to contain over a million tiny pieces.

STATUES & PORTRAITS

the 30-second history

The Romans were deeply

interested in commemorating both the living and the dead. The erection of a portrait statue in a suitable place—for example, a forum for a local politician or emperor, a library for an author—was one of Roman society's highest expressions of honor and success. Over time, many Roman towns acquired a population of marble and bronze figures to supplement their human inhabitants, creating a canon of local and imperial worthies for the ambitious to join. This Roman passion for portraiture probably developed out of the custom of keeping funeral images of illustrious ancestors in aristocratic houses, and parading them at family funerals to show a long and successful lineage. A tendency to invest certain characteristics of appearance with moral qualities meant that portraits could express ideological ideas, as well as simply looking "realistic" (which the best ones certainly did). The choice of whether to look old and wrinkled (like many "veristic" portraits of republican statesmen) or eternally youthful (like Augustus), clean-shaven (like early emperors) or bearded (like second-century CE emperor Hadrian), nude or dressed in military, civilian, or priestly garb contributed to a visually encoded system of messages and morals.

3-SECOND SURVEY
Realistic-looking statues abounded in the Roman world, filling public streets and buildings, private homes, and gardens.

3-MINUTE EXCAVATION
Not all statues were portraits of named individuals. Rich Romans aspired to collect statues of deities and mythological figures by Greek "old masters," or at least decent copies; most Greek bronze sculpture is known to us only through Roman copies and versions. There were statues for all tastes and budgets, from bigger-than-lifesize down to small garden ornaments, but for many people the only sculpted image they would commission would be the portrait bust on their tomb.

RELATED HISTORIES
See also
TOMBS
page 132

3-SECOND BIOGRAPHIES
PRAXITELES
fl. fourth century BCE
The most famous sculptor of the Greek world, seen as highly collectable by later Romans

ASINIUS POLLIO
ca. 75 BCE–4 CE
Roman politician, man of letters, and the first to make his statue collection public

PLINY THE ELDER
23–79 CE
Roman encyclopedist whose work forms the basis for much of our knowledge of statues

30-SECOND TEXT
Matthew Nicholls

Contact with skilled marble and bronze workers of the Greek world played a part in developing the Roman passion for realistic statuary.

TOMBS

the 30-second history

The sides of roads into Roman towns were densely crowded with tombs, as burial was not permitted within city limits. As in much of Roman life, status and wealth were on display: prominent sites by busy thoroughfares, large, eye-catching tombs, and inscriptions (vital evidence for ancient historians) detailing illustrious careers, were all features of the grandest tombs, imitated down the social scale as resources permitted. Rich carving and arresting designs like pyramids or towers proliferated in the late republic, as leading families jockeyed for position. The aim was to commemorate the deceased and to give their spirits (the *manes*) a dwelling place, often in a family group, with access to ritual offerings of food and drink. Some commemoration of the life of the deceased also seems to have been an aim: many tombs depict the inhabitant's profession or trade. Not everyone could afford such luxury in death. The poor, and even some slaves, banded together in burial clubs to finance *columbaria* ("pigeon-hole" tombs), and later on Christians and Jews excavated the vast warrens of the catacombs: a dignified final resting place was tremendously important for all Romans, though individual beliefs about the existence and nature of the afterlife varied widely.

RELATED HISTORIES
See also
INSCRIPTIONS & GRAFFITI
page 90

DEATH & THE AFTERLIFE
page 110

3-SECOND BIOGRAPHIES
AUGUSTUS
63 BCE–14 CE
Rome's first emperor

30-SECOND TEXT
Matthew Nicholls

3-SECOND SURVEY
A final resting place was important, and could provide a last—and lasting—opportunity to show off with a suitable proclamation of status and wealth.

3-MINUTE EXCAVATION
The world of the dead was not immune to fashion or politics. Some elements of burial remained consistent, such as inscriptions giving name, family relationships, and rank or profession. Others changed: Rome shifted from inhumation to cremation early on, and back again in the second to third centuries CE. Changes could be abrupt—Augustus's enormous mausoleum put an end to elaborate funeral architecture, forcing elite families to avoid charges of competing with the emperor by using simpler designs.

Rome's cemeteries contain the mortal remains of both rich and poor, but the tombs of the wealthy could be conspicuously immoderate, many with elaborate architectural forms and inscriptions.

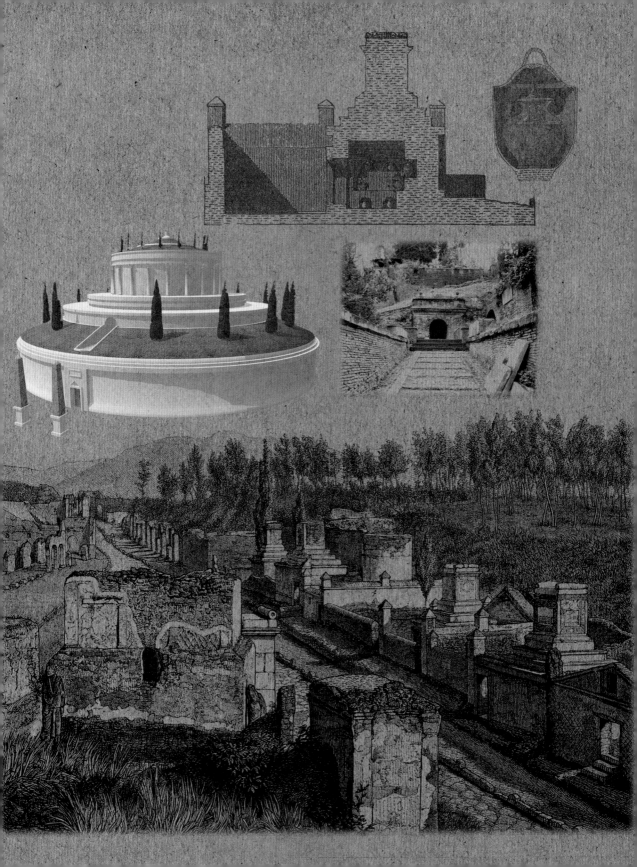

BUILDINGS & TECHNOLOGY

BUILDINGS & TECHNOLOGY
GLOSSARY

army terms The Roman army's composition and strength varied over time, but during much of the Roman empire it fielded a total of about 30 legions. Each legion consisted of heavy infantry legionary soldiers and non-citizen auxiliary troops. There would also be a wing of mounted cavalry. Each legion contained a number of tactical subdivisions: ten cohorts (except the double-strength first cohort) containing six centuries of 80 men each, commanded by centurions. At the lowest level of command legionaries were organized into eight-man tent parties called *contubernium*, commanded by a *decanus*. The whole system helped to foster comradeship and a sense of unit and legion loyalty.

atrium The quadrangular reception hallway that articulated the front part of a Roman town house, with rooms opening off it and a rainwater pool in the center.

ballista, carroballista A torsion-powered artillery weapon that could hurl an iron-tipped bolt or stone projectile over hundreds of yards. Could be used as a siege weapon along with battering rams and siege towers. A carroballista was a cart-mounted version.

caldarium One of the hottest rooms in a Roman bathhouse, heated by hypocausts and wall ducts.

circumvallation A fortification built around a besieged town to increase the besieging army's stranglehold.

Cloaca Maxima The main sewer of Rome, built in the sixth century BCE to drain the marshes land of the Forum area into the Tiber River.

concrete One of the great Roman contributions to architecture: a versatile, robust material that can be molded into any shape and even made to set underwater.

cursus publicus Rome's official system of messengers and couriers, created by the first emperor Augustus to speed links between the provinces and the capital. Supported by way stations along Rome's network of excellent roads, a really important message could travel at up to 50 miles (80 km) per day.

hydraulic gradient The optimum slope of an aqueduct, calculated by Roman engineers to deliver water from a mountain source to a city, without it flowing too quickly or slowly along the way. Often surveyed over distance in difficult terrain with astonishing precision.

hypocaust A system of heating, using hot air from a furnace flowing between pillars that supported a suspended concrete floor, and through ceramic box tiles set into the walls. Typically the hypocaust was used in bathhouses and richer private homes.

insula (pl. insulae) A multistory apartment block that was the most common type of dwelling in ancient Rome. First-floor shops and restaurants opened onto the street, with apartments above.

palaestra An enclosed courtyard, typically part of a gymnasium or bathhouse, used for wrestling and other forms of physical exercise.

pumice A very lightweight volcanic stone.

pozzolana A volcanic ash used by Romans in the manufacture of concrete, mixed with lime.

siege engines As well as *ballista* and *carroballista*, Roman army engineers could construct tall towers, circumvallation walls, and make use of battering rams to overcome enemy defenses.

siphon A device to make water in an aqueduct flow uphill: by channeling water under pressure in lead pipes, Roman engineers could let it flow down one side of a valley and run up the other to return to the proper hydraulic gradient.

thermae A Roman bathhouse; usually refers to the largest imperial bath complexes in Rome. These were truly enormous complexes, with facilities for bathing, strolling, athletics, and more.

tubuli Hollow box tiles set into the walls of heated rooms to draw hot furnace air.

vault An arched ceiling or roof. Roman vaults were built of concrete; shapes ranged from simple semicircular barrel vaults up to complex intersecting designs.

villa A Roman word for house that could be applied to buildings ranging from relatively modest town houses up to the great, luxurious country estates of the rich.

FORTIFICATIONS

the 30-second history

The Roman army's fortifications, near-identical across the empire, show that it had—like many successful armies—a taste for habit and regularity. The classic Roman fort of the first and second centuries CE was the so-called "playing card" type, a rectangle with rounded corners whose ditches and ramparts enclosed a neat grid of streets. In these the various elements of the military would find their proper places—a headquarters in the center, a hospital, stores and workshops, and barrack blocks for the various units of infantry and cavalry. Ovens and latrine pits would serve the daily needs of the soldiers and, in long-term forts, a bathhouse would provide cleanliness and relaxation. The proper layout of these camps developed into a military science, documented by writers like Pseudo-Hyginus. Later Roman forts displayed greater defensive capabilities, as the empire's enemies became a serious threat. Once Rome's expansion slowed down, her frontiers started to harden, and long linear fortifications like Hadrian's Wall demarcated Roman territory (though their exact function—military obstacle or customs barrier—is disputed). Cities, including Rome itself, also acquired imposing wall circuits from the late third century CE, though these, in the end, could not keep the barbarians out.

3-SECOND SURVEY
From Scotland to Africa to Syria, the Roman army's well-built, regular fortresses marked the presence of the legions.

3-MINUTE EXCAVATION
In the early empire, Roman forts—temporary earth and timber structures or more permanent stone ones—were often bases of operation for mobile, aggressive armies. From the third century CE, as the empire's frontiers became more fixed and its internal politics more turbulent, forts acquired more elaborate defensive measures such as projecting towers with artillery platforms. The last great achievement of Roman defensive architecture was the massive Theodosian land walls of Constantinople, which served the city up to its fall in 1453 CE.

RELATED HISTORIES
See also
THE ROMAN LEGION
page 28

THE ROMAN LEGIONARY
page 30

BATHS & HYPOCAUST
page 146

3-SECOND BIOGRAPHY
PSEUDO-HYGINUS
probably third century CE
Name conventionally given to the author of a detailed description of life in the Roman military camp, *De Munitionibus Castrorum*.

30-SECOND TEXT
Matthew Nicholls

Territorial defenses, be they temporary camps or permanent fortresses, almost always used a geometric arrangement of ditches, a rampart, and a palisade.

ROMAN ARTILLERY & SIEGE WEAPONRY

the 30-second history

The Roman army made good use of artillery and siege engines. These had been developed by the engineers of rival Greek kingdoms from the fourth century BCE onward, and were adopted by the rising power of Rome around the middle of the third century BCE. Torsion-powered artillery pieces could launch projectiles—simple rocks or flaming missiles—with considerable range, power, and accuracy. By the imperial period Rome's legions were using compact, mobile bolt-throwing ballistae for infantry support in the field (55 per legion, according to the military writer Vegetius), and heavy-duty stone-hurling catapults for protracted siege operations. Such sieges involved impressive military engineering. The Roman army under Titus laying siege to Jerusalem to suppress a Jewish revolt in 70 CE, for example, built siege towers to give protected fighting access to defensive city walls, and catapults and battering rams to break them down. At the last rebel stronghold of Masada the tenth legion built a circumvallation wall around the sheer clifftop location of the citadel and then a 375-ft (115-m) siege ramp to bring the engines of war up to the rebel defences: the writer Josephus records that the remaining inhabitants committed mass suicide rather than face capture by Roman soldiers.

3-SECOND SURVEY
Rome's military engineers developed sophisticated siege and artillery weapons, and wrote technical treatises to ensure their proper use.

3-MINUTE EXCAVATION
The energy stored by twisted rope or animal sinew could be harnessed to propel a missile at high speed. By mounting twin torsion mechanisms on an iron frame, with long arms connected to a bowstring winched back into position, Roman engineers created the terrifying *ballista*. This weapon could strike from a long distance, demoralizing enemy troops before they had a chance to engage. Standardized, easily replaced components and a portable design added typical touches of Roman efficiency.

RELATED HISTORIES
See also
THE ROMAN LEGIONARY
page 30

FORTIFICATIONS
page 138

3-SECOND BIOGRAPHIES
TITUS
39–81 CE
Military commander (later emperor) who successfully captured Jerusalem and son and heir of emperor Vespasian

JOSEPHUS
ca. 37–100 CE
Jewish aristocrat and leader of the 60s CE uprising who went over to the Romans, prophesied the rise of future emperor, the general Vespasian, and went into honorable exile in Rome, where he wrote histories of the war and the Jewish people

30-SECOND TEXT
Matthew Nicholls

Precise and deadly, Roman mechanized weaponry represented the finest technology of the ancient world.

VITRUVIUS

Vitruvius was a military engineer under Julius Caesar, and a practising architect. Little is known of his life or career (even his full name is lost to us), but his book *De Architectura* ("On Architecture") survives, drawing on both his own experience and on earlier Greek technical treatises. It was written in an era when Vitruvius's patron, the first emperor, Augustus, was transforming the city of Rome "from brick to marble," and enlisting the help of loyalist aristocrats.

According to Vitruvius, an architect needed to be be competent in a wide variety of fields, so his seminal work also helps to preserve insights into mathematics, philosophy, and science, largely drawn from Greek models that are otherwise lost to us—he seems to have sought to make the practice and appreciation of architecture intellectually respectable for a Roman readership steeped in Greek culture, rather than to write a practical handbook for use on a building site.

Vitruvius's work, divided into ten books, covers the training and intellectual formation of the architect, the laying-out of towns, building materials, various categories of building (religious, domestic, and civic), decoration, water supply, mathematics and geometry, and, in book ten, the design of military and civilian machines, including catapults and cranes.

De Architectura's original drawings were lost as the work was copied and recopied through the Middle Ages and beyond. This limitation, and the difficulty of interpreting Vitruvius's complicated text without them, did not stop his work becoming something of a bible for Renaissance architects and thinkers, who followed Vitruvius's insistence on "solidity, usefulness, and beauty" and regular proportions on a human scale.

Later, as archaeologists began to investigate the remains of actual Roman buildings, it was possible to see where Vitruvius's opinion reflected, or departed from, real fashions and tastes in Roman architecture. He is aware of some "modern" developments—concrete, elaborate theater architecture and architectural fresco painting—and tends to mistrust or disapprove of them. Contemporary and later Roman builders paid little heed, however, embracing ever more elaborate forms that would have appalled Vitruvius. His work is best seen, then, as a product of a particular mind and time rather than a comprehensive impartial survey of Roman architectural practice.

Matthew Nicholls

HOUSING

the 30-second history

Housing in the Roman world, as today, addressed people's practical need for shelter and also offered a venue for social display and the expression of individual taste. Roman aristocrats enjoyed town houses on the prestigious Palatine Hill and near the Forum, as well as country estates that combined luxury accommodation and gardens with productive farmland. The smaller properties of less well-to-do Romans are naturally less prominent in the literary record. The first really good evidence comes from Pompeii, where the basic villa style of house, with rooms radiating from a central atrium or hallway, sometimes with a walled garden beyond, covers a huge range of size, prestige, and luxury. Small houses imitate the features of larger ones, which in turn look to the genuinely luxurious aristocratic villas of the nearby Bay of Naples. Where owners had the money, luxury touches like mosaic and fresco, often portraying mythological or literary themes, evoked the world of art and culture. In larger, more densely populated cities like Rome itself, landlords built upward, creating multistory brick apartment blocks known as *insulae*. With shops and restaurants at street level, and reasonably gracious apartments on the second floor, the upper stories of these buildings were notorious for cheap, cramped accommodation.

3-SECOND SURVEY
From gracious villas to cramped top-floor flats, Roman housing reflected the variety of life—rich and poor—across the empire.

3-MINUTE EXCAVATION
Our understanding of life in the "typical" Roman house is clouded by several factors. The Roman empire spanned a huge range of space and time, with varying levels of wealth. The surviving literary record is that of authors (mostly rich Romans) whose texts largely focus on their own houses, ignoring living conditions among the poor or those outside Rome. Finally, archaeological remains in Pompeii, Ostia, and elsewhere, excellent as they are, reveal little about density of occupation or quality of life.

RELATED HISTORIES
See also
LIFE IN THE ROMAN PROVINCES
page 48

MOSAIC & FRESCO
page 128

3-SECOND BIOGRAPHIES
LUCULLUS
118–57 BCE
Politician and consul renowned for his luxury villas and for the fabled Gardens of Lucullus

TRIMALCHIO
1st-century CE
Fictional character in Petronius's *Satyrica*, a millionaire freedman whose house is derided as the epitome of bad taste

30-SECOND TEXT
Matthew Nicholls

From the private retreats of emperors, like Hadrian's island study, to the cramped top-floor rooms of the poor, Roman housing varied enormously with wealth and location.

BATHS & HYPOCAUST

the 30-second history

Bathing was a central part of Roman urban life. While cities like Rome contained hundreds of small private bathhouses, it was in the enormous public *thermae*, built by successive emperors, that bathhouse architecture reached its zenith. Several Roman technologies underpinned these bathhouses. The development of vaulted concrete architecture made huge, soaring spaces possible (and avoided the use of roofing timbers, which would have rotted in the steamy environment). Aqueducts delivered copious water to feed baths, pools, and fountains. Roman transport systems enabled the delivery of huge quantities of decorative marble from across the empire and the regular provision of fuel for heating, made possible by the development of "hypocaust" systems that circulated furnace-heated air under floors suspended on piles of brick or tile. Later, special hollow bricks (*tubuli*) were built into the walls of hot rooms (*caldaria*), to diffuse the heat to the wall surfaces as well. Such systems were common in public bathhouses, where furnaces also heated water in large lead boilers to allow suites of baths at different temperatures, and in the richest private houses.

3-SECOND BIOGRAPHY
SERGIUS ORATA
First century BCE
Architect in the Roman republic who specialized in luxury hydraulic engineering: he invented artificial pools for raising oysters and also heated swimming baths.

30-SECOND TEXT
Matthew Nicholls

Developed from the Greek gymnasium, the Roman bath added the pleasure of copious running, heated water and luxury decoration.

ROADS

the 30-second history

All roads lead to Rome. The power of the city and its emperors over the distant provinces of the empire, and the vitality of the economy, depended on being able to move people, goods, and information swiftly and safely. Straight, direct routes were preferred: these sped the passage of soldiers in a military emergency, and (like aqueducts) signaled Roman domination over natural and human geography. The Romans surveyed the routes of these straight roads with considerable skill, calculating lines between points out of sight of one other and aware of the constraints of the landscape and geology. Once a route was chosen, roads were built to a tried and tested formula. A trench was dug along the line of the road, and filled with compacted coarse gravel. Finer gravel then polygonal blocks of hardwearing basalt formed the road surface, which had a camber for drainage and curbs, milestones, and in towns pavements and stepping stones. Cuttings, embankments, bridges, viaducts, and even tunnels could be built, along with drains and ditches. Roman roads were intended to take two vehicles abreast, and were provided with passing places, way stations—even a network of imperial messengers to carry official dispatches.

3-SECOND SURVEY
Roman roads were highways not just for the army, but also for ideas, laws, and culture, helping to spread Roman ways of life into the provinces.

3-MINUTE EXCAVATION
Roman determination to stick to a direct route could lead to spectacular feats of engineering—mountain routes, such as those in the Alps, could require cuttings of up to 6oft (18 m), and retaining walls and terraces of similar height. The Romans took pride in such achievements: imposing arches were often built as monumental start and end points to these roads. The inscription on the arch at Rimini praises the emperor Augustus for "the numerous roads of Italy sustained by his planning and authority."

3-SECOND BIOGRAPHIES
APPIUS CLAUDIUS CAECUS
340–273 BCE
Roman magistrate responsible, in 312 BCE, for first section of the Via Appia, one of Rome's earliest highways

TRAJAN
53–117 CE
Emperor (ruled 98–117 CE) responsible for huge road construction projects including the Via Nova Traiana in the Middle East

30-SECOND TEXT
Matthew Nicholls

A formidable road-building program endowed the empire with a communications network unsurpassed until modern times.

AQUEDUCTS & SEWERS

the 30-second history

Flowing water was a hallmark of the Roman city. When urban population demands grew too large to be satisfied by local supplies from rivers, cisterns, and wells, aqueducts were built to transport water over great distances. Their rows of arches spanning the landscape remain a visual symbol of Roman engineering expertise. Rome acquired its first, impressive 10-mile (16-km) long aqueduct as early as 312 BCE. Over the centuries the city gained several more aqueducts, bringing water from distant mountain springs and running mostly underground, then on arcades in the approaches to Rome to keep the water at a useful height above ground level. Water ran from distribution towers in pressurized lead pipes to public and private buildings (affluent citizens could pay for a domestic supply; innumerable street fountains served the poor). Used water had to be removed: the Romans built drains to flush waste out of the city, beginning with the seventh-century BCE Cloaca Maxima to drain the Forum. Networks of covered drains carrying waste below street level made some Roman cities comparatively pleasant and hygienic—although ambitious politicians sometimes had to be urged to prioritize their construction over more conspicuous monuments.

3-SECOND SURVEY
What have the Romans ever done for us? Abundant water and an underground network of drains make a powerful case for the civilizing force of the Roman empire.

3-MINUTE EXCAVATION
Were Roman aqueducts useful tools of urban expansion and public health, or wasteful vanity projects designed to embellish their cities with frivolous luxuries like fountains and bathhouses? Both positions have been argued, but modern research is increasingly viewing the channels, arcades, cisterns, settlement tanks, stopcocks, water pipe networks, and siphons built by the Romans as important and sophisticated landmarks in the history of urban civilization.

RELATED HISTORIES
See also
BATHS & HYPOCAUST
page 146

3-SECOND BIOGRAPHY
TARQUINIUS PRISCUS
616–579 BCE
Legendary fifth king of Rome under whose reign work was carried out on the Cloaca Maxima, Rome's "Giant Sewer"

30-SECOND TEXT
Matthew Nicholls

Aqueducts—together with running water, indoor plumbing, and sewer systems—stand as enduring testament to Roman engineering.

CONCRETE & VAULT

the 30-second history

The development of concrete

was one of the most important Roman contributions to architecture, allowing vastly more rapid and economical construction and new types of building. Early Roman concrete consisted of fist-sized pieces of stone ("aggregate") set into a cement mortar, mixed with *pozzolana*, volcanic sandy ash that added strength and consistency. Roman builders used concrete extensively from the third century BCE, experimenting with different facing materials until by the first century CE they were regularly using bricks, made in their millions in brickyards outside Rome. Their efficient building system maximized the use of unskilled and semiskilled labor—transporting materials, making bricks, mixing and laying concrete—allowing the Romans to build huge, virtually indestructible concrete buildings in record time: just six years or so in the case of the Baths of Caracalla. The concrete vault—laid over wooden centering that was removed once the concrete has cured—is a distinctively Roman architectural device. From simple early domes to the huge spans of the Pantheon and imperial bathhouses, and elaborate umbrella- and pumpkin-shaped vaults, such vaults added an architecture of curved, interior volumes to the massive rectilinear, external forms inherited from the Greeks.

RELATED HISTORIES
See also
THE COLOSSEUM & CIRCUS MAXIMUS
page 118

BATHS & HYPOCAUST
page 146

3-SECOND SURVEY
Cheap, flexible, and capable of being laid in massive foundations and walls, and in graceful vaulted shapes, concrete transformed Roman architecture and construction methods.

3-MINUTE EXCAVATION
Concrete can support heavier loads and span wider gaps than the stone architecture of the Greeks, allowing freestanding buildings of enormous size and complexity. Architects grew increasingly bold with their dome designs, using pumice stone as aggregate to lighten the structure at the top, and imitating the ribbed curves of gourds. Even emperor Hadrian may have had a go, if we can believe the story that his court architect told him dismissively to "go away and draw [his] pumpkins."

3-SECOND BIOGRAPHIES
APOLLODORUS OF DAMASCUS
fl. early second century CE
Engineer and architect from Greek-speaking Syria, responsible for many of the finest buildings of Roman emperor Trajan, and master of concrete construction and the vault

30-SECOND TEXT
Matthew Nicholls

The Romans' ability to make concrete led to different architectural forms—huge harbors, wide-span bridges, and soaring vaulted ceilings.

RESOURCES

BOOKS

*Ancient Literacies: The
Culture of Reading in Greece and Rome*
William A. Johnson and Holt N. Parker
(Oxford University Press, 2009)

Augustus: Image and Substance
Barbara Levick
(Longman/Pearson, 2010)

*The Cambridge Companion to
Ancient Rhetoric*
Eric Gunderson
(Cambridge University Press, 2009)

Classics: A Very Short Introduction
Mary Beard and John Henderson
(Oxford University Press, 2000)

Latin Fiction: The Latin Novel in Context
Heinz Hofmann
(Routledge, 1999)

The Legacy of Rome: A New Appraisal
Richard Jenkyns
(Oxford University Press, 1992)

*Literate Education in the Hellenistic and
Roman Worlds*
Teresa Morgan
(Cambridge University Press, 1998)

The Oxford History of the Classical World
John Boardman, Jasper Griffin and
Oswyn Murray
(Oxford University Press, 1986)

Roman Declamation
Michael Winterbottom
(Bristol Classical Press, 1998)

*Roman Eloquence: Rhetoric in Society and
Literature*
William J. Dominik
(Routledge, 1997)

*Roman Historiography: An Introduction to its
Basic Aspects and Development* Andreas
Mehl and Hans-Friedrich Mueller
(Wiley-Blackwell Publishing, 2011)

Roman Imperial Architecture
J.B. Ward-Perkins
(Yale University Press, 1994)

Roman Villas in Central Italy
Annalisa Marzano
(Brill, 2007)

Rome. An Oxford Archaeological Guide
Amanda Claridge
(Oxford University Press, 2010)

ARTICLES

Houghton, L. (2013) *Ovid, remedia amoris 95: uerba dat omnis amor*. Classical Quarterly, 63 (1). pp. 447–449

Hunt, A. (2012) *Keeping the memory alive: the physical continuity of the ficus Ruminalis* in Bommas, M., Harrisson, J. & Roy, P. (eds.) *Memory and Urban Religion in the Ancient World* (London) pp. 111–128

Kruschwitz, P., Campbell, V., and Nicholls, M. (2012) *Menedemerumenus: tracing the routes of Pompeian graffiti writers*. Tyche, 27. pp. 93–111

Lowe, D. *Always Already Ancient: Ruins in the Virtual World* in Kretschmer, M., Thorsen, T.S., & Wahlgren, S., (eds.), *Virtual Worlds of Classics: A Guide* (Tapir: 2012) pp. 53–90

Marzano, A. (2013) *Agricultural production in the hinterland of Rome: wine and olive oil*. In Bowman, A.K. and Wilson, A.I. (eds.) *The Roman agricultural economy: organisation, investment and production*. Oxford University Press, Oxford, pp. 85–106

Nicholls, M. *Galen and libraries in the Peri Alupias, Journal of Roman Studies*. 101. pp. 123–142

WEB SITES

Centre for the Study of Ancient Documents
www.csad.ox.ac.uk

Project website about the ancient marble map of Rome
www.formaurbis.stanford.edu

Harbour City of Ancient Rome
www.ostia-antica.org

Range of ancient texts in the original languages and translations, and searchable versions of several older reference works
www.penelope.uchicago.edu/Thayer/E/Roman/home

Online resource covering history, literature and culture of the Greco-Roman world
www.perseus.tufts.edu

Large collection of images of Pompeii
www.pompeiiinpictures.com

Website about Matthew Nicholls' digital modelling project
www.reading.ac.uk/classics/research/Virtual-Rome.aspx

Roman Aqueducts
www.romanaqueducts.info

NOTES ON CONTRIBUTORS

EDITOR

Dr Matthew Nicholls studied at Oxford University and is a senior lecturer in Classics at the University of Reading, where he specializes in books, libraries, cities, and monuments of the Roman world. He directs Reading's MA City of Rome course and is also producing a digital model of the entire ancient city.

Luke Houghton has taught Latin, Greek, and Classics at the Universities of Glasgow and Cambridge and at University College London, and has held visiting fellowships at the British School at Rome and the Warburg Institute in London. He has published articles, notes, and reviews on Roman poetry and its reception in later art and literature (principally in the late Middle Ages and early Renaissance), and has edited books on the poet Horace and on Renaissance Latin poetry.

Ailsa Hunt is the Isaac Newton Research Fellow in Classics at Fitzwilliam College, Cambridge. Her primary research interests are in Roman religion. Ailsa also edits the annual magazine *Tellus*.

Peter Kruschwitz is Professor of Classics at the University of Reading. He is one of the leading experts in Latin linguistics, Roman metre, Latin verse inscriptions (the so-called Carmina Latina Epigraphica), Roman comedy (most notably Plautus and Terence), and the wall inscriptions of Pompeii and Herculaneum. Previously, Peter was a member of the research staff of the *Corpus Inscriptionum Latinarum* at the Berlin-Brandenburgische Akademie der Wissenschaften, before obtaining a prestigious two-year Emmy Noether scholarship of the Deutsche Forschungsgemeinschaft. He is a former Visiting Fellow of All Souls College, Oxford, and is a Fellow of the Royal Historical Society.

Dunstan Lowe is a Lecturer in Latin Literature at the University of Kent. He has published on various topics in Roman culture and literature, especially Virgil, Ovid, and other poets of the Augustan period. He is also interested in how contemporary popular culture responds to classical antiquity, especially in newer media such as video games, and was co-editor (with Kim Shahabudin) of the book *Classics for All: Re-Presenting Antiquity in Mass Cultural Media* (Cambridge Scholars Publishing, 2009).

Annalisa Marzano is Professor of Ancient History in the Classics Department at the University of Reading, a Fellow of the Society of Antiquaries of London, and a Fellow of the Royal Historical Society. Her research focuses on Roman social and economic history and on Roman archaeology. She took part in many archaeological projects investigating Etruscan, Greek, and Romans sites in Italy, Libya, and Egypt. She is the author of two monographs, *Roman Villas in Central Italy* (Brill, 2007) and *Harvesting the Sea: The Exploitation of Marine Resources in the Roman Mediterranean* (OUP, 2013). She directs the University of Reading MA in Ancient Maritime Trade.

Susanne Turner is Curator of the Museum of Classical Archaeology at Cambridge. She has a special interest in classical sculpture and its viewers—male and female, rich and poor, ancient and modern.

INDEX

ACKNOWLEDGMENTS

PICTURE CREDITS
The publisher would like to thank the following individuals and organizations for their kind permission to reproduce the images in this book. Every effort has been made to acknowledge the pictures; however, we apologize if there are any unintentional omissions.

All images from Shutterstock, Inc./www.shutterstock.com and Clipart Images/www.clipart.com unless stated.

Borghese Collection: 124.
Corbis/Araldo de Luca: 89TL.
Alberto Fernandez Fernandez: 45C.
Flickr/Iessi: 45.
A Hunter Wright: 84.

Remi Jouan: 79.
Matthias Kabel: 31R.
Jaakko Luttinen: 119.
Marie-Lan Nguyen: 97, 102, 111, 131.
Matthew Nicholls: 81, 133.
Till Niermann: 25, 42, 83.
Pascal Radigue: 39B.
Wolfgang Sauber: 64.
David Shankbone: 139.
Ulysses K. Vestal: 81.
Walters Art Museum: 101B.
Wikipedia/Basilio: 27C; Bertramz: 27B; Carlomorino: 105B; Godot13: 141; Pippo-b: 133; Sailko: 21L, 63, 83, 105C; Shakko: 21R, 79; WKnight94: 77; Zanner: 29.